D0966552

WHO READS POETRY

WHO
50 VIEWS FROM
READS
POETRY MAGAZINE
POETRY

Edited by Fred Sasaki
and Don Share

UNIVERSITY OF CHICAGO PRESS
Chicago and London

Poetry magazine was founded in Chicago by Harriet Monroe in 1912 and is the oldest monthly devoted to verse in the English-speaking world. Monroe's "open door" policy, set forth in volume 1 of the magazine, remains the most succinct statement of *Poetry*'s mission: to print the best poetry written today, in whatever style, genre, or approach.

Please visit poetrymagazine.org to access the entire series, The View from Here.

The University of Chicago Press, Chicago 60637
The University of Chicago Press, Ltd., London

Printed in the United States of America

25 24 23 22 21 20 19 18 17   1 2 3 4 5 6 7 8 9

ISBN-13: 978-0-226-50476-6 (cloth)
ISBN-13: 978-0-226-50493-3 (e-book)

Library of Congress Cataloging-in-Publication Data

Names: Sasaki, Fred, editor. | Share, Don, 1957– editor.
Title: Who reads poetry : 50 views from Poetry magazine / edited by Fred Sasaki and Don Share.
Description: Chicago ; London : University of Chicago Press, 2017. | Includes index.
Identifiers: LCCN 2017030355 | ISBN 9780226504766 (cloth : alk. paper) | ISBN 9780226504933 (e-book)
Subjects: LCSH: Poetry—History and criticism. | Poetry (Chicago, Ill.)
Classification: LCC PN1055 .W53 2017 | DDC 808.1—dc23
LC record available at https://lccn.loc.gov/2017030355

♾ This paper meets the requirements of ANSI/NISO Z39.48-1992 (Permanence of Paper).

For Harriet Monroe

Poetry is such a delicate, pretty lady with a candy exoskeleton on the outside of her crepe-paper dress. I am an awkward, heavy-handed mule of a high school dropout. I guess I just need permission to be in the same room with poetry.

NEKO CASE

I will never understand why more people don't appreciate poetry. Even when I am confounded by a poem, it changes my world in some way.

ROXANE GAY

CONTENTS

INTRODUCTION

Poetry can occur anywhere there are words, even in daily life.

IAIN MCGILCHRIST

Poetry in daily life may seem an extravagant thought, as if "poetry" and "daily life" are somehow opposed to each other, difficult to reconcile—as if we have another life in which to find poetry. Poets themselves have brought up such a division—for example, Yeats, who famously described the necessity of choosing between the "life" and the "work." Anyone can see that you don't have one without the other, yet there's a noble and appealingly romantic sense that poetry is something elevated, that it's aloof, floating on extended wings above the quotidian: that life has one kind of reality, and poetry another. Is it so? When I talk to people about poetry, which I do all the time, I often hear things like "Oh, I read some poetry in school, even wrote a bit of it, but I don't have time for it now." I'll be unhesitatingly told that poetry *today* is written so that nobody can understand it, except maybe other poets. And in the media, where poetry itself is scarcely encountered day to day, one repeatedly and unavoidably encounters fervid articles that ask outright, "Is poetry dead?" or worse, "Is poetry irrelevant?" So much for Ezra Pound's saying that poetry is news that stays news!

The quotation I take as my epigraph comes from a "View" written by a psychiatrist, whose daily professional life involves understanding the kinds of connections people make. Like poets, psychiatrists are interested in deep perception and, ultimately, metaphors. As McGilchrist wrote elsewhere in *Poetry*'s pages, "For me everything depends on the reciprocal relationship between our minds and the relatively independent world beyond them." There: the connection between poetry and daily life. I suppose many people imagine poets to be on the crazier end of the sanity spectrum, and perhaps many are. Yet it is possible, indeed necessary, for a therapist like McGilchrist to read poems the way he reads patients; talking about the Philip Larkin poem "Coming," he writes, "Here the intimations of recovery and forgiveness, coming out of suffering and desolation, and also of a deep bareness out of which something unimaginably rich is to come—for a while—are subtle and complex."

The tension between life and what can be imagined is creative, and it's necessary. As Kay Redfield Jamison, professor of psychiatry at the Johns Hopkins School of Medicine, says, putting it more intimately, "I have found a kind of solace in poetry that I cannot find elsewhere."

People seek solace all their lives, but poetry often addresses things seemingly more mundane than that—for instance, the seeking of wealth. Money, after all, is a kind of metaphor, and one that everybody understands well. "I'm an economist. Yet poetry is my first stop on the way to invention—discovery of metaphors," wrote Stephen T. Ziliak in his "View." For Ziliak, poetry is all about economy, in the sense of efficiency: think haiku, with a budget of three lines. He considers, in his piece, the "dominant metaphor" of economics, the "invisible hand," and asks whether poets can help the economy—a good, and seldom asked, question.

The work of the invisible hand is traceable not only in economics but in our own health. When the philosopher Richard Rorty was diagnosed with inoperable pancreatic cancer, his family gathered around him.

> My cousin (who is a Baptist minister) asked me whether I had found my thoughts turning toward religious topics, and I said no. "Well, what about philosophy?" my son asked. "No," I replied, neither the philosophy I had written nor that which I had read seemed to have any particular bearing on my situation. . . . "Hasn't *anything* you've read been of any use?" my son persisted. "Yes," I found myself blurting out, "poetry."

Rorty's conclusion: "I now wish that I had spent somewhat more of my life with verse." Rorty is not alone in wishing so. The late film critic Roger Ebert, in one of his last published pieces, shows how all through his life poems "simply found a place for themselves, and they stayed."

As you'll see in this book, other kinds of labor connect deeply and fruitfully with poetry. Josh Warn worked for twenty-nine years as an ironworker. As he points out, "Ironwork is often artful enough, if not arty, and there are reasons that carrying longish poems in memory has some of the same satisfactions as completing a difficult weld or fitting a steel handrail to a curved stair."

Lieutenant General William James Lennox Jr. served as the fifty-sixth superintendent of the United States Military Academy at West Point. He observes that, "like warfare, poetry can result from the collision between romance and reality." Note that here an opposition between "real life" and the imagination is fatal. Poetry is taught at West Point, and when PBS anchor Jeffrey Brown visited a classroom there, as he describes in his piece in this book, he affirmed that "discussions of the role of poetry in our society can feel irrelevant or abstract. Not in [a] West Point classroom."

But how did these views come to be published in *Poetry*? Christian Wiman, who was its editor for a decade, and who has likely spent more time with poetry than anyone else alive, expressed the concern that "poets often spend their entire poetic lives around universities, [and] the whole enterprise seems to have high walls around it. Poets determine what gets published. Poets review other poets. Poets give each other prizes." Those sentences appeared in *Poetry*'s January 2005 issue by way of introducing a new feature called The View from Here. Only the view wasn't, as that title might seem to imply, going to be the view from the editor's chair.

Wiman devised a feature of the magazine—ingeniously stewarded by *Poetry*'s Fred Sasaki and from which all these "Views" are taken—that would serve as an ongoing riposte to the charges against poetry and open up the landscape by enlisting writers from *outside* the poetry world to write about it.[1] In fact, what Wiman said

1. It's no coincidence that I use the word *riposte* here, for that was the title of a book of twenty-five poems published the very month and year *Poetry* was born: October 1912. Its author was Ezra Pound, who was also the magazine's first (and only) foreign correspondent, known for bringing to our pages the likes of T. S. Eliot and Rabindranath Tagore. So our riposting has a history as old as we are. As you might expect, Pound himself had a few things to say about the professionalization of poetry. In a 1930 essay called "Small

a decade ago remains strikingly true: poetry has indeed become professionalized in this country. The critic Mark McGurl claims in his book *The Program Era: Postwar Fiction and the Rise of Creative Writing* that the MFA has been the single greatest influence on American literature since World War II, noting, as the *New York Times* put it, that "most serious writers since then have come out of graduate-school incubators." A similar career track is rapidly being followed in the United Kingdom. Note that this is a career path, not a road to success. You don't need a degree to write, of course, and having one guarantees nothing, not even a job. What seems clear despite all this is that people from walks of life *outside* the profession of poetry are, as Wiman pointedly observed, "perfectly qualified to judge anything now being written. And what seems even clearer is that, if you're a poet writing today, these are the readers you want."

. . .

As I've already suggested, a number of these readers are included in this collection: doctors, professors, journalists, politicians. As you would expect, musicians and actors can be deeply affected by poetry. "My mother was a poem written by Gwendolyn Brooks," as Grammy and Academy Award–winner Rhymefest boldly puts it in his view. The actress Lili Taylor says, "Poetry has helped me become more versed, so to speak, in the language of emotion." When it comes to writers, even novelists need poetry. Pinkaj Mishra wrote that he reads it "for the same reason I read prose fiction: for a brief escape into a reality more comforting than the one I lived in."

Music, movies, and novels all provide escape, and so too do sports. Poetry and athletics have gone hand in hand since antiquity, from Pindar's odes to the present day, when Kobe Bryant announced his retirement in verse. And as Major League Baseball player Fernando Perez writes, "Like poetry, baseball is a kind of counterculture." In this sense poetry isn't in any sort of opposition to life but runs *counter* to it (a fine distinction).

Magazines," he writes: "The public runs hither and thither with transitory pleasures and underlying dissatisfactions; the specialists say: 'This isn't literature.' And a deal of vain discussion ensues." You can see that this question of "professionalization" goes back to *Poetry*'s—and modernist poetry's—very beginning, and it hasn't gone away.

Even politicians, whose mantra lately is that "you campaign in poetry, but you *govern in prose*," turn to poetry.

This suggests that poetry has a beneficial effect. It may well have, but more than anything, poetry is a pleasure. In each of the pieces in this book, you'll notice that, different as each writer is from the others, they all have one thing in common: they take enormous pleasure in poetry. How can this be?

I'd say that the best answer might be found in the artist Ai Weiwei's "View": "To experience poetry is to see over and above reality. It is to discover that which is beyond the physical, to experience another life and another level of feeling. It is to wonder about the world, to understand the nature of people and, most importantly, to be shared with another, old or young, known or unknown." This describes something pleasurable and wonderful, but also vast. I suspect that vastness goes a long way toward explaining why people might have some trouble, at first, with poetry. Neko Case goes so far as to tremble before the muse: "I guess I just need permission to be in the same room with poetry." But poetry is in the same room with us, whether we know it or not, as the pages that follow show. In these brief essays people from all walks of life will keep you in superb company as you work out your own views of poetry, and suggest the many ways poetry accompanies us in daily life and in our own work.

Don Share

Poetry has helped me become more versed, so to speak, in the language of emotion.

LILI TAYLOR

Poetry teaches me that I basically know nothing, and that acknowledging this position is a beginning and never an end.

JIA TOLENTINO

RICHARD RAPPORT is clinical professor of neurosurgery at the University of Washington's School of Medicine and the author of *Nerve Endings: The Discovery of the Synapse* and *Physician: The Life of Paul Besson.*

IT IS NOTHING LIKE THAT

Though most days are an easy routine, people who spend their lives in operating rooms know that something awful is only one burst blood vessel, one uncontrolled infection, one random biological reversal away from ending a perfectly contented life. Our biochemistry makes sure things work well most of the time. But then, what are the possibilities for any two strands of DNA to become entwined? The lurking of chance that gives one person a ruptured aneurysm at twenty-five while permitting another to develop comfortable habits and drop dead at eighty-nine is what makes the poetics of doctoring.

When chance seized the teacher, football player, poet—and my patient—Richard Blessing, he was a lot like me: early forties, athletic, a reader, in love with his life. And then one day as he forced a graduate student to go to his left on the basketball court, a convulsion dropped Professor Blessing to the hardwood. Boom. A successful, happy life had turned into a sad one. Difficult, painful, short.

After eighteen months of his illness, Dick paid very close attention to words. CT scan, MRI, tumor, biopsy, radiation, and chemo are the vocabulary of the sick; because of his nature, the words circulated around the tumor in Dick's brain and came out as poems. What I said to him rattled around in there too. I was out of town when he suddenly got worse. "Is it now?" he asked. "Maybe," I told him from that other coast. "Probably." When I got back to Seattle two days later he was comatose, rolled up on his side facing a wall, eyes closed. He stayed that way for a week.

Then he woke up and lived another year.

His collection *A Closed Book* includes a short poem titled "Directions for Dying." This title wasn't rhetorical, of course. I couldn't save him, a man of my own age and habits. Was I useless? Was there no justice? Well, no. Much of biology is chance and cannot be altered or avoided even by the acceptance of some infinite force outside of space and time. Medicine only alters the course of things slightly. Doctors have wonderfully exact therapies to influence some diseases, but not all. We don't treat many cancers very well, or genetic diseases, or age. And treatment, of course, isn't the same as cure. Sometimes the best treatments are nothing but advice and comfort.

While my reading of prose has helped me understand much that I didn't know, poetry is a way to better see the things I might know deep down but cannot (or will not) say. Poems create empathy. The person with the knife in hand requires a better understanding of "maybe" than the training provides. While contemporary people, and perhaps surgeons in particular, tend to believe that they are in charge of their destiny and the fate of others, in truth we are adrift in a universe only partially visible to us, and we insist on guessing about the rest of it. Camus said that physicists were reduced to poetry— and that was before string theory. Denise Levertov called our handle on life in the universe "this great unknowing." In her late poem, "Primary Wonder," she writes about the mystery that there is anything, anything at all—let alone *everything*.

It is this everything that poetry helps reveal in our operating rooms and clinics. One task of medicine is to predict the direction of chance, to help patients prepare for what will probably happen. But that's so small a part of why people consult doctors. What about what could happen, or should happen, or might not? What about the ambush of the least likely? Isaac Babel wrote that the essence of art is unexpectedness, and it is in these side channels of life where poetry is a better guide than a textbook.

Forty years ago, when I was in medical school, I believed in this work as science. But clinical medicine has become a business of technology, not science. The latter is a way of looking at the universe. The former is method functioning within established statistical rules. And method may be industrialized. It is very difficult to jam into the same mind an industrial worldview and a humanistic one, which is why many medical schools now have formed departments of "humanities in medicine." It really is love and work that define our communal life: medical students and residents must learn that. Young people learning to be doctors require poets. It is poetry that shows them, as Dick Blessing wrote regarding his own approaching death, that

> It is not like entering a mirror nor like closing a door
> Nor like going to sleep in a hammock of bones.
> You may expect what you like. It is nothing like that.

HANK WILLIS THOMAS is a photo-conceptual artist whose work is in numerous public collections including the Museum of Modern Art, the Solomon R. Guggenheim Museum, and the Whitney Museum of American Art.

BETTER SPEAK

My first meaningful interaction with poets came as a young adult when my friends and I would frequent open mics at poetry cafés in New York and DC. There are two defining moments. First, my mother, Deborah Willis, invited poet Sekou Sundiata to perform his opus *The Circle Unbroken Is a Hard Bop* at the Smithsonian. Soon after that my friend Nekisha gave me a mixtape of spoken word that included Nikki Giovanni's "The Way I Feel" and the Watts Prophets' "Rapping Black." I was in awe of the courage and shameless earnestness and vulnerability in their work. I felt the sharp contrast between the optimism and determination of the civil rights generation and the oblique nihilism of mine. They all but indicted the listeners for remaining silent or irreverent when times called for social or moral action.

A few years later I encountered Audre Lorde's "Litany for Survival." The last few lines are emblazoned on my soul:

> and when we speak we are afraid
> our words will not be heard
> nor welcomed
> but when we are silent
> we are still afraid
>
> So it is better to speak
> remembering
> we were never meant to survive.

"Better to speak!" echoes in my mind whenever I feel like shriveling up and hiding in the corner rather than being exposed or critiqued. There is sheer audacity required to write words for a broader audience, even more to get up and read those words aloud. I feel the same is true for contemporary visual artists. To speak is almost to say "I know," but in most cases artists are speaking about things they don't know, or are still in the *process* of knowing. I feel like poetry is at its best when it speaks to this process of knowing, dangling on your heart right before it gets to your mind.

So much of my practice is a collaboration with audiences and other artists—sometimes it's overt, sometimes subversive. As it happens, I was introduced to the notion of collaboration by Kamal Sinclair (now a collaborator of mine on *Question Bridge: Black Males*) who worked with a combination of poets, dancers, and musicians to write a multifaceted off-Broadway stage show called *The Beat*. It was a come-as-you-are and leave-your-heart-on-the-stage experience. That was around the time Danny Hoch wrote *Jails, Hospitals and Hip Hop*. I saw the written word translated into spoken word as activism.

And then there is Saul Williams, whom I first encountered on a student film shoot at NYU in the late nineties. It was an adaptation of Baldwin's "Sonny's Blues." Saul was Sonny. After two days I was basically a disciple. I'll never forget the moment he picked up a kalimba (African thumb piano) off a coffee table on set. He strummed it a bit, then turned it over and found an old Burger King sticker on it. He said, "Now that's deeper than all of us," and put it down. Not two years later I was creating work about commodity culture as it related to African American history and culture.

Without a doubt, the best text-based work of mine came from an adaptation of an iconic sign from the civil rights era that read "I am a man." I was always amazed by the power of the image of a large group of African American men holding signs to affirm their "manhood." It also seemed to exemplify the fissure between my generation and my parents' generation. After all, the phrase we used was "I am the man." How did we go from a collective statement under the repression of segregation to an apparently selfish statement for a generation "liberated" by integration?

I wanted to explore that, so I created a series of twenty paintings in which I riffed on the syntax of the sign. The paintings were then arranged into a poem format with the help of a songwriter named Sparlha Swa. The last ten of them read "I'm the man, who's the man, you the man, what a man, I am man, I am Human, I am many, I am am I, I am I am, I am. Amen." Rather than judge or validate myself on anyone else's standards, maybe my greatest gift is my own consciousness. I am. Amen. Or as Langston Hughes put it,

So since I'm still here livin',
I guess I will live on.
I could've died for love—
But for livin' I was born

Though you may hear me holler,
And you may see me cry—
I'll be dogged, sweet baby,
If you gonna see me die.

Life is fine!
Fine as wine!
Life is fine!

from "Life Is Fine"

LILI TAYLOR is a stage and screen actress. Her film credits include *Short Cuts*, *I Shot Andy Warhol*, and *The Conjuring*. She has appeared in *Six Feet Under* and, recently, *American Crime*.

OUT THERE

I was suffering from Weltschmerz one day (translation: woe for the world). My chest was hurting.

I call my dear friend Marie (the poet Marie Howe).

"Marie, my heart hurts."

"You have Jack Gilbert's *Refusing Heaven*, right? There's a poem at the beginning. I can't remember the name. The first line is something like, 'sorrow everywhere.' Read it to me."

> Sorrow everywhere. Slaughter everywhere. If babies
> are not starving someplace, they are starving
> somewhere else. With flies in their nostrils.
> But we enjoy our lives because that's what God wants.
>
> from "A Brief for the Defense"

I finish reading the poem. Neither one of us says anything for a moment. Breathe. I look up. I see a tree through the window. I hear a robin singing. I see the sky. Clouds gently moving.

A poet told me that the job description of the poet is to say the unsayable. Another poet said no matter which way you cut it poems are about emotion. They are about deep emotion.

My work (acting) involves emotions. How do I translate the emotions into something actable? How do I sort through them? Specify and name them? A poet once told me that originally the poet's job was to name things of this world.

In a way, I am trying to name things with my emotions.

When I begin work on a script I go from the beginning and distill each scene down to its essence. And then I try to name each scene with a word or two or more. It's almost as if I'm trying to write a poem for each scene, articulating the inchoate, indescribable, unknowable. So I go through the script and I go through and through it, with my mind and without it. Much the same way as when I'm reading a poem. And then I put the script down when the play or movie begins. Good acting, like a good poem, remains mysterious to me. I couldn't *tell* you what it means, but I know it.

I used to try so hard to understand a poem. I was being vigilant instead of receptive. If the poem is saying the unsayable, I don't need to articulate it back to myself with words. The poet has done that for me. If poems are about emotions, then that is the language I need to use when I'm reading them. Poetry has helped me become more versed, so to speak, in the language of emotion.

I would be thrilled if I could be as "out there" with my acting as poets are with their poems. Leaping toward the stuff that is bubbling around us, unseen but felt. It's uncharted and raw—a kind of pure, undiluted matter brought back for those who want it:

> This sky like an infinite tenderness, I have caught
> glimpses of that, often, so often, and never yet have
> I described it, I can't, somehow, I never will.
>
> How is it that I didn't spend my whole life being happy,
>   loving
> other human beings' faces.
>
> And wave after wave, the ocean smells like lilacs in
> late August.

from *Walking to Martha's Vineyard*, by Franz Wright

Biological anthropologist HELEN FISHER is a Fellow at the Kinsey Institute and a member of the Center for Human Evolutionary Studies at Rutgers University. Her books include *Anatomy of Love*, *Why We Love*, and *Why Him? Why Her?*

THE MADNESS OF THE GODS

I study the brain in love. My colleagues and I have put forty-nine people who were madly in love into a brain scanner (fMRI). Seventeen had just fallen happily in love; fifteen had just been rejected in love; seventeen were men and women in their fifties who maintained they were still "in love" with their spouse after an average of twenty-one years of marriage. All showed activity in a tiny factory near the base of the brain that pumps out dopamine, the neural liquor that gives you the energy, focus, craving, and motivation associated with intense romantic passion—what the ancient Greeks called "the madness of the gods."

But before I launched these brain-scanning projects, I searched the academic literature for the constellation of psychological symptoms linked with romantic love. More exciting to me, I also read poetry from around the world. As other anthropologists have studied fossils, arrowheads, or potsherds to understand human thought, I studied poetry to understand the lover's besotted brain. I wasn't disappointed: everywhere, poets have described the emotional fallout produced by the brain's eruptions as one becomes engulfed with romantic fervor.

Take "special meaning": as you fall in love, you begin to regard your beloved as special, unique, unlike any other. "Juliet is the sun," Romeo exclaims. The Indian poet Kabir writes, "The lane of love is narrow—there is room for only one." And in *The Jade Goddess*, the twelfth-century Chinese fable, Chang Po says to his beloved, "Since heaven and earth were created, you were made for me and I will not let you go." Then the lover begins to dote on every tiny aspect of the beloved. Most can list what they do *not* like about their sweetheart. But they sweep these details aside to concentrate on what they adore. The car the beloved drives is different from every other car in the parking lot. The street this person lives on, the music he listens to, the books she reads: everything related to the beloved grips the lover's attention. As the ninth-century Chinese poet Yuan Chen wrote,

> I cannot bear to put away
> the bamboo sleeping mat:
> that night I brought you home,
> I watched you roll it out.

"Love is blynd al day," says Chaucer, and as the passion grows, this brain bath of dopamine fills the lover with restless energy, euphoria when things are going well, mood swings into despair when shunned. "This whirlwind, this delirium of Eros," Robert Lowell called it. Bodily responses accompany this mental storm. Ono No Komachi, a ninth-century female Japanese poet, wrote, "I lie awake, hot / the growing fires of passion / bursting, blazing in my heart." These bodily insurrections—from butterflies in the stomach to sweaty palms, weak knees, and a pounding heart—are probably the result of norepinephrine, a chemical closely related to dopamine.

So begins a physical and mental addiction to another human being, an addiction often portrayed in verse. "O, I willingly stake all for you," were Whitman's words. And an anonymous eighth-century Japanese poet summed up this craving: "My longing has no time when it ceases." But I think Plato best expressed what is happening in the lover's brain. In *The Symposium* he writes that the God of Love "lives in a state of need." Romantic love is a need, a want, a craving, a homeostatic imbalance, a *drive* that arises from primitive regions of the mammalian brain, giving us the energy, focus, and motivation to win a mating partner—life's greatest prize.

In fact, I think romantic love is one of three different brain systems that evolved for reproduction. The *sex drive* urges us to seek a range of partners; *romantic love* motivates us to focus our mating energy on just one individual at a time; and feelings of *attachment* enable us to remain with this person at least long enough to raise a single child through infancy together. Each kind of love is associated with different primary brain chemicals and brain pathways; each evolved to spread our DNA on toward eternity. But of these three basic reproductive drives, romantic love is the best described—perhaps because dopamine is linked with creativity. And as this chemical courses through the brain, it produces the sleeplessness, energy, and imaginative fire that drive the impassioned lover to compose.

"Mind is primarily a verb," wrote philosopher John Dewey. The mind *does* things. And poets capture these workings of the brain with words, enabling me to touch, feel, and understand some of the complex emotions that the brain produces as we fall in love.

NATALIE Y. MOORE is a reporter for WBEZ-Chicago. Her latest book is *The South Side: A Portrait of Chicago and American Segregation*.

LOVE JONES

When we were children, my mother would gather my two siblings and me for story time. Occasionally she read us poetry. I remember when she introduced us to Paul Laurence Dunbar. "In the Morning" quickly became a favorite and is one of my earliest poetry memories.

> 'LIAS! 'Lias! Bless de Lawd!
> Don' you know de day's erbroad?
> Ef you don' git up, you scamp,
> Dey'll be trouble in dis camp.
> Tink I gwine to let you sleep
> W'ile I meks yo' boa'd an' keep?
> Dat's a putty howdy-do-
> Don' you hyeah me, 'Lias -you?

My younger brother Joey and sister Megan and I loved Dunbar's use of black dialect. We took turns reading stanzas aloud, cracking up at whoever this 'Lias person was getting fussed at so early in the morning. Megan recited the poem anytime she had to perform an oratory contest.

I grew up on the South Side of Chicago in sort of a black middle class racial cocoon. We had black-owned businesses in proximity and strong block clubs. My parents filled our childhood with messages of black uplift and positive images to counter the prevailing mainstream narrative about African Americans. Our exposure to African American literature came from my mother. Learning about black poets and writers nurtured me and let me know I, too, could be a writer. When either my sister or I have a bad day, we joke, "Life for me ain't been no crystal stair," a line from a Langston Hughes poem we learned early on.

Poetry changes for me depending on what I need. I can't count the number of times I heard little ones perform Useni Eugene Perkins's "Hey Black Child" at talent shows. Chicago native Perkins is a poet and youth activist influenced by the Black Arts Movement of the 1960s. He served as executive director of the Better Boys Foundation of Chicago social services agency. Working with youth informed his writing. He wanted teens to soar above stereotypes served up by Hollywood. Perkins's plays exalted Ida B. Wells and Paul Robeson.

Hey Black Child
Do you know who you are?
Who you really are
Do you know you can be?
What you want to be

If you try to be
What you can be
Hey Black Child!
Do you know where you are going?
Where you're really going

I took acting classes at a black theater, which furthered those messages of uplift. As a teenager, my go-to monologue came from Ntozake Shange's choreopoem *for colored girls who have considered suicide/when the rainbow is enuf*. I pretended to be grown à la Lady in Red.

one thing I don't need

is any more apologies
i got sorry greetin me at my front door
you can keep yrs
i don't know what to do wit em
they don't open doors
or bring the sun back
they don't make me happy

or get a mornin paper
didn't nobody stop usin my tears to wash cars
cuz a sorry.

When I attended college in the 1990s, the coffeehouse/jazz/poetry scene flourished. The movie *Love Jones*, whose lead character writes poetry, reflected the smoke-hazed mood. Unfortunately, in real life much of the poetry sucked—from people who used open mics as a pick-up schtick to those who made Hallmark card writers seem prolific. Throw in some perfunctory "motherland" militant pieces and oversexed erotica under a bed of audience snaps. I say this not out of snobbery but because back then I thought I *needed* to write poetry. It fit the boho writer aesthetic I craved. So much so it became a joke to my family that I only dated dreadlocked poets. (Not true. Yet my father and older male cousin frequently said I needed to stop dating those poetry readers. They laughed; I rolled my eyes.)

After standing up once in front of a warm coffeehouse crowd, I realized I need not ever do that again. No one booed. In fact, they clapped. But I vowed to stay in my journalistic writing lane following that open mic experience. Poetry appealed to what I projected a writer to be, which was no more realistic than the secluded cabins on the lake that people think all writers have. Once free of that fictive notion, I could appreciate poetry and look to it as a nonfiction writer for lyrical inspiration, simplicity and loveliness. Or cheekiness. The tagline on my personal email is a Nikki Giovanni quote: "I'm so hip, even my errors are correct."

More than a decade later I participated in the local humanities program. My good friend and poet Alice led the workshop in which we riffed off a Gwendolyn Brooks poem. "We are each other's harvest; we are each other's business; we are each other's magnitude and bond." In small groups we discussed how we are each other's business in a racially segregated city like Chicago. I loved how poetry helped bond us in that moment.

I've turned to Alice many times since then to help me find poetic words. When writing my latest book, *The South Side: A Portrait of Chicago and American Segregation*, I asked Alice to recommend a passage about the meaning of home, because sometimes poetry does what I can't. She found Maya Angelou's *All God's Children Need*

Traveling Shoes. "The ache for home lives in all of us, the safe place where we can go as we are and not be questioned."

I recently had a baby and at my shower friends and family created a keepsake book with pearls of wisdom. Alice tapped into Maya Angelou again and wrote in gold cursive: "Love recognizes no barriers. It jumps hurdles, leaps fences, penetrates walls to arrive at its destination full of hope."

Another reminder that we are each other's business, and proof that poetry can fill the sentiment when one is searching for the right words.

Now that I have a new baby girl, I hope to repeat what my mother did for me with black poets. Now I just have to decide which poem I read to her first. I'm leaning toward Maya Angelou.

This is the highest purpose of poetry, or song:
It keeps us from listening to fools.

LEOPOLD FROEHLICH

Poetry isn't just a way of writing, it's a way of thinking.

MARY SCHMICH

ROGER EBERT (1942–2013) was a journalist, screenwriter, and film critic for the *Chicago Sun-Times* from 1967 until his death. In 1975 he was the first film critic to win the Pulitzer Prize for Criticism.

ALL MY HEART FOR SPEECH

Many lines of poetry are so long-embedded in my memory that I find them appearing when I speak or write. Sometimes I am quoting. Sometimes I am unconsciously drawing from the reservoir. Some poets lend themselves to that, because they have found a way to say something important in words that seem almost inevitable. These words for the most part I made no effort to memorize. They simply found a place for themselves, and they stayed.

One poem I deliberately set out to memorize. In the eighth grade Sister Rosanne required us all to learn a poem by heart. I was assigned "To a Waterfowl," by William Cullen Bryant. For years thereafter I regaled listeners with as much of it as they desired:

> Whither, 'midst falling dew,
> While glow the heavens with the last steps of day,
> Far, through their rosy depths, dost thou pursue
> Thy solitary way?

The only other poet whose work I memorized was E. E. Cummings, because he called out to be heard aloud. That process happened naturally because I read so many of his poems aloud so many times. My undergraduate mentor Daniel Curley told us Cummings's typography could act as a guide to reading aloud. In my interpretation it resulted in readings a great deal more spirited than Cummings's own businesslike dispatches.

I heard him in a reading once at the University of Illinois. The small bald man with wise eyes was introduced by Curley, came onstage, sat in a chair behind a table that held a water pitcher, a glass, a microphone, and a manila folder of copies of the poems he planned to read. He regarded us.

"I will begin," he announced, "and read for about forty minutes. There will be an intermission. Then I will come back out and read for about half an hour more. There will be no questions."

He read his work as I have heard him read it on recordings. Dry. A brittle lyricism. No attempt to sell or underline the language. He treated it as factual.

I'd always imagined the poems more like songs. At the University of Cape Town in 1965, I actually did a performance of Cummings at a smoky, quasi-beatnik campus coffee shop, although that was hardly the start of a performing career.

The great performer of poetry in my life has been Bill Nack, a classmate at the University of Illinois. Bill later went on to become a much-honored senior writer at *Sports Illustrated* and the biographer of Secretariat, but to this day he's always memorizing a new poem or prose passage. When we were freshmen he presented me with the last page of *The Great Gatsby*—and followed it with the first page, which is not so commonly heard.

Bill can go indefinitely, and he would whenever we met. That inspired my career as an impresario. I devised a program titled "A Concert in Words" for Bill to perform at the annual Conference on World Affairs at the University of Colorado in Boulder, and again after dinner one night at Rancho la Puerta, a spa we are both fond of in Tecate, Mexico. I wasn't surprised that the campus event drew a big crowd, but I had my doubts about Rancho. After rising at dawn for a mountain hike, were these people ready for poetry after dinner?

We filled a room. Bill dimmed the lights a little and read for an hour, mostly standing in front of the podium without a book. The campers demanded an encore. He read for another thirty minutes. Then he got a standing ovation and they marched on the concierge to demand a second performance. He read the next afternoon for another hour. His selections included Nabokov, Frost, Eliot, Yeats, and Cummings, of course. They enjoyed poetry more than they realized.

I envy him his energy and his love of the words. He brings a fresh nonacademic enthusiasm to his performances. I think he stirs a dormant love of language in many people, in these days when so much flat and lifeless prose is published. Is it unthinkable that today's grade schools require the memorization of a poem or two? Sister Rosanne assured us we would thank her in later years. When I meet old classmates from those years, I find she was correct.

Another friend of a lifetime is John McHugh, who was born in Sligo, Ireland—Yeats Country. When we met in the late sixties he was a reporter at the *Chicago Daily News* (where Carl Sandburg had once been the film critic), and I was at the *Chicago Sun-Times*. John had apparently ingested Yeats in volume, and often on late beery nights he would recite him at O'Rourke's Pub in Chicago.

I remembered more of it than I realized. One night at the Telluride Film Festival, I was pressed into service to do an onstage interview with Peter O'Toole. We covered many of his films and adventures, and then I said, "I understand you have always wanted to play Jack Yeats."

This was true, and he responded to it with a line or two by W. B. Yeats. They jarred something within me, and I answered with a few more lines of Yeats. Our eyes met, and something clicked. He quoted some more Yeats, and then I did, and we went on for ten minutes or so, and he laughed and said, "Well, I think we've done our job."

ARCHIE RAND is professor of art at Brooklyn College. His work is displayed around the world, including in the collections of the San Francisco Museum of Modern Art, the Art Institute of Chicago, the Victoria and Albert Museum, and the Tel Aviv Museum of Art.

THEY COULD CROON

In elementary school we memorized Longfellow, Poe, Kipling, Whitman, Browning, and dozens of others. I've always appreciated that. My high school clique recited "Moody's Mood for Love" and Annie Ross's "Twisted" as hazing for hipness. I smoked Camels, carried Sartre, read Ginsberg, Crane, Stevens. I was a Beat-lite confection.

The first day of class my freshman year at City College I met Ross Feld. He said, "What do you do?" I said, "I'm a painter, what do you do?" He said, "I'm a poet." I'd never met anyone who called himself a poet. I thought that was pretty sharp. Ross introduced me to Williams, Pound, Zukofsky, Spicer, and other poets of current interest to him. The New Directions imprint became my symbol of Kashruth, allowing me to read anything between those boards. In the bars and at readings my mentors included Gil Sorrentino, Amiri Baraka (LeRoi Jones), Joel Oppenheimer, Fielding Dawson, and Paul Blackburn. Even in reading Moyshe Leyb-Halpern I found a voice similar in directive to Sorrentino's and William Bronk's and Basil Bunting's: a willed, adult tempo, a conviction so palpable that it could redeem by intonation alone.

Eventually I discovered a good use for this stuff. I have done many painting and drawing series employing text as an equal visual element. While drawing a group of books that incorporated a Clark Coolidge poem, I realized the printed words against the image returned visually, they resounded and shaped the picture, that, in this opera, DaPonte could be Mozart. John Yau and I have engaged in jousting on paper and canvas for twenty years. I must give credit—it was his idea. We have made a household industry of our collaboration, and I love to work with him. Our collective pile officially considers itself flip, but I suspect the radio beeps are signaling a depth of more measure than we gambled on. We don't talk about it. Only divine retribution will make our collaborations popular, but I find our shenanigans edifying.

I met John Ashbery in the mid-seventies through David Kermani, who was my director at the Tibor de Nagy Gallery. As a young painter I would work on uncut bolts of canvas, reinserting chunks of story into the inlay, and Ashbery's work was instructive, corroborating, for me. His rhythm was one I sympathetically associated with the discoveries of Jackson Pollock, John Coltrane, and Cecil Taylor, and I had always wanted to work with him. David informed me that John was working on a poem, "Heavenly Days," which might be appropriate for our collaboration. I decided that the remarkable Ashbery house in Hudson, New York, was the source of the voice in this poem, and I made numerous trips to paint the interiors. A bemused John watched as I needed to include just one more angle or subject to complete our forty-seven-chapter project. When I handed the pile back, Spielbergian effects transformed the paintings as John wrote on them. Philadelphia-proper acrylic paintings took on names like *The drain choked with tumbleweed* or *others avoid laxatives and beef* or *They could croon* or *The philosopher is your boyfriend*. Only the greatest poets can supply what reconstitutes us. What more effective gift could there be than validation for our own relentlessness?

At a younger moment Robert Creeley's "I Know a Man" was the most important poem I knew. Creeley writes the great humanist poems of our time. When I take out my own garbage, or when Seinfeld says "Tampax," I know Creeley's concern has been here first. I need the poems. I am dependent on the poems. They help me out in a jam. If you check anyone's medicine cabinet—anyone's—you'll find Creeley poems behind the Sudafed and scissors.

I first met Creeley through the painter Dan Rice. I would ask friends of mine in the circles of Diane di Prima and Denise Levertov to reintroduce me in bars and at St. Mark's Church. I made an animated film accompanied by texts from "Pieces." It was John Yau who first thought of a collaboration between Creeley and me, and it was John who made it happen. For a work called *Drawn & Quartered* I prepared fifty-four plates on which I had loosely drawn turn-of-the-century-type illustrations. I felt the articulation of event would accommodate the location in Creeley's speech, although the specific characters could prod him slightly off his coordinates. Confident in the strength of the drawings and not aware of the conceit in my proposition, I was content to let Bob respond. I sent Xeroxes of images, but I was not ready for the gut-crunching answers he rattled off on the spot. My drawings were asked to talk instead of preen. And he made them do it. I have gratitude for the wisdom gained and the product created. Fine songsmiths we turned out to be. In my studio now I wonder if that painting over there can pass a polygraph, something I thought I had always been asking myself.

LEOPOLD FROEHLICH is a senior editor at *Lapham's Quarterly*. Previously he was the managing editor of *Playboy* magazine.

ONE-TRACK MIND

My job as a magazine editor requires a fair amount of travel. I console myself during these trips by listening to an iPod. From the moment I hail a cab until the moment I approach a hotel desk, the iPod plays constantly. I use it to shut out the world.

During the course of these travels, I have developed a compulsion of listening over and over to one track. I played Darrell Scott's "This Beggar's Heart" fifty times in a row. There is a character in one of Thomas Bernhard's novels who listens incessantly to Beethoven's Third Symphony, the phonograph arm returning throughout the night to the beginning of the record. I've done that. I've listened to Hans Knappertsbusch conducting the "Marcia Funebre" again and again on a flight somewhere.

This is a form of madness, yet I prefer to believe that song flourishes on refrain. We hear things in a thirtieth listen that were not there during the first twenty-nine. There is comfort in familiarity, in knowing exactly which note will play next. And there are many glorious moments worth hearing a thousand times, like Oumar Sow's guitar solo, which rises unexpectedly three and a half minutes into Cheikh Lô's "N'Dawsile."

Which brings me to my point. My friend Amy gave me *The Caedmon Poetry Collection*, three CDs of poets reading their own work, which I loaded on my iPod. I am always glad when a poem plays. William Carlos Williams shows up on shuffle at Sea-Tac, reading "The Seafarer," or Gertrude Stein appears out of the blue in Pittsburgh, declaiming "If I Told Him: A Completed Portrait of Picasso."

After one ridiculous trip to Los Angeles, I flew back to Chicago—a three-and-a-half-hour journey—listening to Joseph Brodsky read George Kline's translation of his "Nature Morte." The poem clocks in at 4:17, so it must have been repeated fifty times as the plane crawled across the continent.

I will admit to some confusion about the poet's words. Brodsky described his English as "better for reading and listening than for speaking." What I heard in his weary threnody was song: I was compelled by the sound of his voice. I found his Russian accent familiar and soothing. I was moved by the cadence and lilt of his recitation.

When I got home I dug out my volume of Brodsky and read the poem. I discovered that I had misheard a number of phrases, and the text clarified a few of my uncertainties.[1] But that mattered little.

To hear "Nature Morte" is to hear song, a song as old and immutable as blind Homer. "The song was there before the story," said Brodsky, who was indeed a singer.

I am dismayed when I hear questions about the utility of poetry. How do you use poetry, and what is it good for? This is odd. Poetry is song. No one asks, What use is song? What use are birds? Poetry has no use. It matters because of its inutility.

"Poetry is not a form of entertainment," wrote Brodsky, "and in a certain sense not even a form of art, but our anthropological, genetic goal, our linguistic, evolutionary beacon."

People go out of their way to ignore this beacon today, but they do so at their own peril. "By failing to read or listen to poets," Brodsky wrote in "An Immodest Proposal," "a society dooms itself to inferior modes of articulation—of the politician, or the salesman, or the charlatan—in short, to its own."

Maybe Brodsky had this right, and this is the highest purpose of poetry, or song: it keeps us from listening to fools.

1. Isaiah Berlin tells of a 1990 lecture Brodsky gave at the British Academy: "No one understood a thing . . . nor did I. He was speaking English quickly, swallowing his words. And I couldn't catch it, couldn't quite understand what he was saying. Listening to him was enjoyable, because he was animated, but I didn't understand until afterwards, when I read [the text]."

NAOMI BECKWITH is a curator at the Museum of Contemporary Art in Chicago. She has curated several exhibitions in the United States and internationally.

THE NECESSARY FLUSTER

Though I do not have a "favorite" of many things, I do have a favorite poem: Elizabeth Bishop's "One Art." Its words on loss are so even keeled for five stanzas that I immediately became a devotee of its matronly, metaphysical advice. But suddenly, in the sixth stanza, the poem cracks open, leaking vulnerability. I love the poem for its timeless subject, its progression, and especially its title, which I consider a pun on my own professional interests as a curator. When I mentioned this to an English professor friend, he commanded that I recite "One Art" like a pop quiz. I consented and got through four lines until my friend interrupted me—"Elizabeth Bishop would never use the word *fluster.*" An argument ensued, Google was consulted, and eventually I was vindicated.

Our argument was essentially an academic one about Bishop's practice, but it mirrored ongoing debates about what type of language and forms are appropriate for poetry. In this case "fluster" was common, colloquial, too close to slang, and, for my friend, inconsistent with Bishop's lyricism. It's as if poetry's only function were embellished erudition.

My own notions about what constitutes poetry veer toward the decorative as well, but when I think back on the poetry that first grabbed my imagination—"We real cool. We / Left school"—its diction was akin to slang. The monosyllabic words, the idiosyncratic meter, the creative verbs (to "Jazz June"?): these weren't simple aesthetic choices for Gwendolyn Brooks, they were linguistic portraits. Like Brooks, I lived for much of my life on the South Side of Chicago. The familiarity of her cadences primed my young mind for poetry.

The familiar or colloquial isn't base but inspirational—and, I would argue, necessary. Over one hundred years prior to "The Pool Players," Charles Baudelaire stated that art must find its inspiration in the urban street, in the everyday, in the nineteenth-century version of the pool hall. Baudelaire was known as much as an art critic as a poet, and his ideas helped engender the cultural shift from the Romantic age into modernism.

Visual art and poetry have continued along separate aesthetic tracks, but I often return to poetry when I think about contemporary visual art. For instance, Kenneth Goldsmith's concept of uncreative writing: Goldsmith—a true heir of Baudelaire's dandyism—advocates for the wholesale borrowing or repurposing of language from any source rather than creating "new" texts. It is a radical notion in a world saturated with clichés and nostalgic references. Goldsmith's view is about making lateral moves rather than justifying what language is appropriate for poetry. It's a vision of language that accepts "fluster."

I also see Goldsmith's ideas in direct conversation with visual art's notion of the "found object." An artist utilizing appropriation or a found object forces her audience to look anew—and critically—at the world. Artists and poets who do this go beyond style to pose conceptual questions: What does it mean to, like Brooks or Baudelaire, engage directly with the world surrounding you rather than looking toward the academy? How do you take advantage of the familiar while making it unfamiliar and surprising? These questions are now my guiding principles as I consider contemporary art.

MARY SCHMICH is a Pulitzer Prize–winning columnist for the *Chicago Tribune* and wrote the *Brenda Starr* comic strip from 1985 to 2011.

POETRY, DAILY

I write a news column at the *Chicago Tribune,* and at the beginning of baseball season this year one of my editors phoned with a tough assignment, something, he said, that called for special skills.

Was I being asked to investigate a doping scandal? Conduct an exclusive interview? Throw out the first pitch?

"Can you write us a poem about opening day?" he asked.

He and I both knew that by poem he meant doggerel—silly verse written with a wink—and I obliged:

> Yes, baseball's back, at last, at last
> To bat away the blues
> The games arrive like sunshine
> In the bleepin' gloomy news.
>
> Blagojevich indicted!
> The economy's a mess!
> Plus parking, potholes, crooks and crimes!
> We need some anti-stress!
>
> from "An Ode to Opening Day"

It ran on the front page, embroidered with old-fashioned bunting that signaled that rhyming verse, like baseball itself, was a relic of a quainter time.

I've always felt slightly sheepish about the pleasure I get from my occasional forays into doggerel. The enjoyment some columnists get from their political fulminations, I get from rhyming "spinach" and "Kucinich."

I feel only slightly less sheepish about how often I exploit the poems of real poets to make a serious point. Poetry and journalism are like peanut butter and baloney: coupling them is not to everyone's taste.

But I can't help myself. Poetry isn't just a way of writing, it's a way of thinking, and I've been thinking that way since at least sixth grade.

At Alexander School IV in Macon, Georgia, Miss Lois Birch, who seemed as old as God, made us memorize poems. The two I remember spring to mind as often as the faces of old friends. I keep them in my head the way you might keep worry beads in your pocket, reaching reflexively in times of stress for their meaning, rhythm, sound.

One is by John Masefield: "I must go down to the seas again, to the lonely sea and the sky, / And all I ask is a tall ship and a star to steer her by." The other is by William Wordsworth:

> I wandered lonely as a cloud
> That floats on high o'er vales and hills,
> When all at once I saw a crowd,
> A host, of golden daffodils.

Since sixth grade, I've memorized poem fragments that range from the wisdom of A. A. Milne ("Where am I going? I don't quite know. / What does it matter where people go?") to the wisdom of Wallace Stevens ("She says 'But in contentment I still feel / The need of some imperishable bliss'").

Whenever I can, I sneak poems into my newspaper column.

After terrorists flew airplanes into the World Trade Center, I instinctively flipped through my most dog-eared book of poems, Wislawa Szymborska's *View with a Grain of Sand*, and plucked a few verses from "Hatred":

> See how efficient it still is,
> how it keeps itself in shape—
> our century's hatred.
> How easily it vaults the tallest obstacles.
> How rapidly it pounces, tracks us down.

Her poem gave my prose a power it wouldn't otherwise have had.

When W. S. Merwin won the 2009 Pulitzer Prize for poetry, I used the occasion as an excuse to quote from "Rain Light," about a mother's death. I put a link to the entire poem on my column, and hundreds of readers sought it out.

I've bolstered my own summer musings with Mary Oliver's "The Summer Day," whose last line electrocutes me every time I read it: "Tell me, what is it you plan to do / with your one wild and precious life?"

In autumn, I've quoted from Pablo Neruda's "October Fullness," though it's about October as a time of life more than a time of year:

> Little by little, and also in great leaps,
> life happened to me,
> and how insignificant this business is.

The response to the columns in which I quote good poems is always strong, which is another reason to feel sheepish: even with full attribution I'm reaping credit for someone else's genius.

Poetry also creeps into *Brenda Starr*, the soap-opera comic strip I've written for twenty-four years. Our heroine, Brenda, quotes poetry and muses on it. Heroes and villains alike use it to woo her.

Recently a mysterious, dashing man named Ringo, from the fictitious country of Kazookistan, dazzled her with verse:

Ringo didn't conquer Brenda, but he did seduce many comics readers who were grateful to discover Rumi and Hafiz.

Newspaper columns, comic strips, and poems may not seem like related literary forms, but they're less different than they look. In their own ways, each of them seeks the same thing: to make meaning in a space whose power lies in always being just a little too short.

JIA TOLENTINO is a staff writer for the *New Yorker* website. Her writing has appeared in the *New York Times Magazine*, *Pitchfork*, and many other places.

KNOWING NOTHING

I spend all day on the Internet, but many of its mandates are alien to me, and none feel quite as strange as this central, self-contradictory, two-part injunction: first, that you should talk all the time—weigh in on things, as if that was our duty—*and*, impossibly, always believe that you are right.

That pressure is becoming increasingly powerful among the people who provide shape to public rhetoric. Print media is mirroring online media; online media is mirroring social media. Some days everything feels like a maelstrom, a series of fights over identity, in which everyone is consistently misrepresenting their own stakes. The danger of writing on the Internet is that you can place too much trust in your own quick opinions, and thereby screw the precious pooch of your own mind. A passing thought needs time in private; there is nothing more suspect than a person in uncomplicated love with what he thinks.

I have taught poetry workshops to two very different groups who prepared me well for the reflexive talkativity and self-righteousness that now dominates the Internet: college freshman, and children between the ages of seven and nine. The first was at the University of Michigan, the second in a scrappy public elementary school in the Fourth Ward of Houston. The syllabi weren't the same, of course, but the kids understood Richard Siken ("Driving, dogs barking, how you get used to it, how you make / the new street yours") and Anne Sexton ("Here / in the room of my life / the objects keep changing"). They could write poems after Charles Simic's shoes and Nikki Giovanni's ego tripping and Richard Brautigan's catfish friend. And with about three exceptions, my favorite poems—the ones that work self-evidently, that compel me to understand a craft I still have no idea how to step inside of, that have penetrated my thick skull with the use of this art form over and over—were those I could teach in both classrooms, to both adult and child.

One of these poems was Louise Glück's "The Red Poppy," which opens with three lines that have become something of an operating principle in my life. The poppy says,

> The great thing
> is not having
> a mind.

As the poem continues, I quibble: the invocation of deep instinct through the conceit of anthropomorphization is one of the few things I feel does not gain clarity through being written down—that is, whenever I have been a wild goose like Mary Oliver and let the soft animal of my body love what it loves and all that, the "it" in question isn't always pretty. But what an opening! I try to live by it. I want instincts over positions, humility over certainty. *The great thing is not having a mind.*

Not that I talk to anyone about poetry, ever. My relationship to it is sidelong and almost entirely private. I can't write it; I read it irregularly. In the practice of teaching it, I could only locate myself as a student, with no authority, no important opinions, no sense that I was ever *correct*.

And that, in the end, is what made me free.

When I write, still, I often feel like one of my third-graders, saying the word "beautiful" and then miming a fishing line cast out into the middle of the classroom because we needed to keep going until we found "hallowed" or "conspicuous," a brighter and fresher fish. When I read closely, I feel like I'm one of my freshmen, counting out the anapests in a rap verse, spending an hour on a single Kendrick Lamar couplet. "This black on black is a blessing / Black on black crime on my weapon," he spits in this one throwaway Jeezy cut, and the way these two lines invert each other's meaning and meter have taught me again and again to be in love with the fact of the basic project of writing. Forget opinions, and certainly forget being *right*: it's enough to have the task of trying to write words that retain their meaning—to learn to distrust whatever comes too easily, and then to reconceive equilibrium yourself, then to reconceive equilibrium, over and over, within a small space.

Poetry taught me how to write everything but poetry. Poetry teaches me that I basically know nothing, and that acknowledging this position is a beginning and never an end. *The great thing is not having a mind.* From a point of nothingness, the world starts to sparkle. It becomes declarable. It brings you those fleeting sensations that are worth sitting on, punching around, forming into ideas that may not be correct, necessarily, but will have some gravity, maybe even feel new.

I'm an economist. Yet poetry is my first stop on the way to invention—discovery of metaphors. No matter the audience, a model is a metaphor.

STEPHEN T. ZILIAK

Perhaps the deepest value of poetry for scientists is its articulation of the feelings that scientists themselves harbor for what they study—passion, deep curiosity, and a sense of stewardship.

NALINI NADKARNI

IAIN MCGILCHRIST is a psychiatrist, philosopher, and former clinical director at the Bethlem Royal and Maudsley Hospital, London. He is author of *The Master and His Emissary: The Divided Brain and the Making of the Western World.*

FOUR WALLS

When I left the world of academic English literature it was not because I was any less passionate about poetry, but because I did not want to spend my life operating on my friends. I thought I might kill them. Later I learned of Ted Hughes's dream about the fox that came to him, singed and smelling of burnt hair, put its paw on the essay he was writing, leaving a bloody mark, and said, "You are destroying us."

Poetry engraves itself in the brain: it doesn't just slip smoothly over the cortex as language normally does. It has all the graininess of life, as it rips into being from deep within the limbic system, the ancient seat of awareness and affective meaning. Sometimes this is most obvious in a foreign language, because there the smooth, familiar words recede, and the sheer awesomeness of what is meant comes refreshed by the new encounter. As a child I was bewitched by the poems of Heine that my father would recite to me while shaving. *Im Abendsonnenschein* . . . I remember thinking then that the real word for sunshine was *Sonnenschein*. So, too, something seemed missing when things disappeared: they only truly disappeared when they were *verschwunden*. This is odd because my father was a Scot and my mother English. It seems like a sort of latent knowledge.

Although I have favorite periods for music and painting, I do not for poetry. Poetry can occur anywhere there are words, even in daily life. After twenty years I still remember the response of a psychotic patient of mine when asked to distinguish between a river and a canal. Without hesitation he responded, "A River is Peace, a Canal is Torment," a line worthy of Blake. The forging of unusual links—metaphor—in which poetry resides depends on the right hemisphere of the brain, where the overall meaning of language, rather than mere syntax and semantics, is appreciated. It is here, too, in the right hemisphere, that experience is fresh, truly present, not predigested into re-presentation.

In adulthood I have found that many of my favorite male poets had a history of mental illness—Blake, Hölderlin, Smart, Cowper, Clare, Hopkins. And, interestingly, each of my favorite female poets—Dickinson, Plath, Charlotte Mew, Stevie Smith—had a history of either mental illness or ambivalent sexuality, or both. Quite apart from the fact that such experience may prove fertile ground for poetry, I wonder if this—and the astonishing prevalence of depression in general amongst poets—points to an anomalous lateralization of brain function, with a right hemisphere bias at the phenomenological level.

In practice as a psychiatrist, listening to the voice of suffering, I find myself often recurring to certain specific lines. Hardly a day goes by when I do not think of Wilfrid Gibson's "the heart-break in the heart of things." And how Larkin understood regret:

> Truly, though our element is time,
> We are not suited to the long perspectives
> Open at each instant of our lives.
> They link us to our losses.

But the sheer terror of depression is for me embodied in the last stanza of Cowper's "The Castaway"—"No voice divine the storm allayed, / No light propitious shone"—or his half-crazed

> Me miserable! how could I escape
> Infinite wrath and infinite despair!
> Whom Death, Earth, Heaven, and Hell consigned to ruin,
> Whose friend was God, but God swore not to aid me!

I myself have suffered with depression, and I remember feeling that the only way I could convey how I felt was through some lines by Hölderlin, who spent the last years of his life in an insane asylum. After two stanzas in which he recounts the blissful eternal life of the gods in Elysium, the poem turns:

But to us who suffer,
to mankind, it is given
to have no place to rest,
blindly we falter and fall
from one hour to the next,
like water that's tossed
from cliff to cliff, down
the years into the unknown.

Ivor Gurney's searing poem "To God" was a later discovery that should be compulsory reading for every psychiatrist. It seems to me to have everything there is to say about psychotic depression, and the utter powerlessness in the face of some brutal force that such patients experience. It is a salutary reminder never to play into that feeling by attempts to help, however well-meaning:

Why have you made life so intolerable
And set me between four walls.

His last words send a chill down my spine, passing, like my father's German verses, Housman's shaving test:

Gone out every bright thing from my mind.
All lost that ever God himself designed.
Not half can be written of cruelty of man, on man.
Not often such evil guessed as between Man and Man.

ROXANE GAY is the author of the books *Ayiti*, *An Untamed State*, *Bad Feminist*, and *Hunger*. She lives and writes in the Midwest, for now.

A PLACE FOR POETRY

Because I am a writer and I teach writing, people expect me to know about poetry. In truth, I know very little about poetry even though I read a great deal of it. I am vaguely familiar with various forms—sestina, sonnet, cinquain, ghazal. I am unfamiliar with the craft of poetics—line break, rhyme, meter, image. What I do know is that when I read poetry, good poetry, I forget to breathe and my body is suffused with something unnameable—a combination of awe and astonishment and the purest of pleasures.

I will never understand why more people don't appreciate poetry. Even when I am confounded by a poem, it changes my world in some way. Poetry makes me think more carefully about the lyricism and the language I use in my prose. It helps give shape to my writing, helps me bring the reader to the heart of what I want to say. Poetry gives me the strength of conviction to take chances in my writing, to allow myself to be vulnerable.

Reading poetry is such a thrill that I often feel like I am getting away with something just to be able to indulge in reading it. That thrill shows me how poetry is in everything.

Take the poem "Trespassing" by Lisa Mecham, a poem about the night wanderings of teenagers, written in couplets. Look at the last two lines: "Then on the plywood floor, it's just a boy pounding away / and a girl, her quiet cries turning stars into doves inside." There is so much captured in that moment—we are given a scene, all too familiar but uniquely rendered, haunting, aching, gorgeous. Or "Cattails," by Nikky Finney, a prose poem: a rush of words, a story of love and distance, a whole world, and the exquisite phrase "she is reminded of what falling in love, without permission, smells like."

Or xTx, the poem "Do You Have a Place for Me," and the unforgettable lines "I will collect your hair / with my mouth / Use the strands / to sew the slices / in my heart." This is a poem I loved so much that I wrote a story with the same title so I could carry it with me forever.

Or take Jericho Brown, telling too much necessary truth in all his work, but especially "Bullet Points," on the violence black men and women experience at the hands of cops. "I promise that if you hear / Of me dead anywhere near / A cop, then that cop killed me." I heard Jericho read this live and found myself on the edge of my seat, my fingers curled into tight, sweaty fists as I tried to absorb the pain wrapped in the intense beauty of his words.

Or Eduardo C. Corral, who rocks as he reads his poetry before an audience, who blends English and Spanish and demands that we, as his readers, keep up. He writes of borders, erasing and challenging those that exist, while erecting new borders of his own. "Ceremonial" is full of hunger and sorrow and eroticism: "His thumbnail / a flake / of sugar / he would not / allow me to swallow."

Or Aimee Nezhukumatathil, who uses poetry to write of the wonders of the natural world. She writes about being brown in white America, about being a daughter, a wife, a mother, of being a woman making sense of her own skin. Her poem "Small Murders" tells of Antony and Cleopatra, Napoleon and Josephine, how scents were woven through their loves: when a new suitor admires her perfume given by another, "by evening's end, I let him have it: twenty-seven kisses / on my neck, twenty-seven small murders of you." The poem ends with the elegant twist of a very sharp knife.

I could write of many more poets and poems that reach into my mind, my body, and never run out of words. There is no shortage of excellent, truly excellent poetry in the world. As I sit here, I am surrounded by books by Jonterri Gadson, Solmaz Sharif, Warsan Shire, and Danez Smith. I can't wait to lose myself in their poetry.

A retired US Army three-star lieutenant general, WILLIAM JAMES LENNOX JR. was superintendent of the United States Military Academy at West Point from 2001 to 2006. He holds a PhD in literature from Princeton University and is currently the president of Saint Leo University.

ROMANCE AND REALITY

As I write this, American soldiers serve in harm's way in places such as Mosul, Fallujah, and Jalalabad. For young leaders in today's army, the war on terror constitutes a difficult and sometimes tragic reality.

Meanwhile, in the small classrooms of West Point, young cadets consider war through the eyes of Rudyard Kipling, Carl Sandburg, and John McCrae. During his or her plebe year, every West Point cadet takes a semester of English literature, reading and discussing poetry from Ovid to Owen, Spenser to Springsteen ("Thunder Road" provides a catalog of poetic devices). Cadets must also recite poems from memory, a challenge that many graduates recall years later as one of their toughest hurdles.

Like warfare, poetry can result from the collision between romance and reality, as the ironic title of Owen's "Dulce et Decorum Est" memorably observes. So too, our new cadets arrive full of romantic idealism, then spend the next forty-seven months at the academy learning the pragmatic realities of discipline, integrity, and leadership.

Why, in an age of increasingly technical and complex warfare, would America's future combat leaders spend sixteen weeks studying the likes of simile, irony, rhyme, and meter? Those who can't communicate can't lead. Poetry, because it describes reality with force and concision, provides an essential tool for effective communication. Like most colleges, West Point emphasizes both verbal and written communication skills, and our faculty evaluates cadets on their substance, style, organization, and correctness. In studying poetry, cadets gain a unique appreciation for the power of language. From alliteration to onomatopoeia, the poet's tools allow words to transcend the limitations of syntax. We may hear that transcendence in Shakespeare's imagery and Whitman's passion, but it is there as well in the closing cadence of MacArthur's farewell: "when I cross the river, my last conscious thoughts will be of the corps, and the corps, and the corps." We do not hold our cadets to this standard of stentorian elegance; we do, however, teach them to appreciate what makes this language different.

Second, poetry confronts cadets with new ideas that challenge their worldview. The West Point curriculum includes poetry, history, philosophy, politics, and law, because these subjects provide a universe of new ideas, different perspectives, competing values, and conflicting emotions. In combat, our graduates face similar challenges: whether to fire at a sniper hiding in a mosque, or how to negotiate agreements between competing tribal leaders. Schoolbook solutions to these problems do not exist; combat leaders must rely on their own morality, their own creativity, their own wits. In teaching cadets poetry, we teach them not what to think, but how to think. Finally, poetry gives our cadets a new and vital way to see the world, a world that many of my generation could not have imagined. When I entered West Point in the summer of 1967, Academy graduates were waging a very cold war in central Europe and a very hot war in the jungles of Southeast Asia. In the thirty-eight years since, countless changes, some magnificent and some tragic, have shaped a very different future for my grandson.

Often these tectonic shifts in history and society resist clear exposition, particularly when these shifts involve armed conflict. Louis Simpson noted this elusiveness when he wrote:

> To a foot soldier, war is almost entirely physical. That is why some men, when they think about war, fall silent. Language seems to falsify physical life and to betray those who have experienced it absolutely—the dead.

Since the *Iliad*, poetry has allowed its writers to capture war's chaos and horror with a power that other artists lacked. One can, for example, read a hundred accounts of the Crimean War, but none of them will convey its pointless barbarity like Tennyson's "Charge of the Light Brigade." Those few stanzas convey the romance and reality of warfare more clearly than any other medium.

We may not produce a poet laureate at the United States Military Academy. If, however, we develop graduates who can communicate clearly, think critically, and appreciate the world through different perspectives, we will provide the army and the nation with better leaders.

STEPHEN T. ZILIAK is professor of economics at Roosevelt University and professor of business and law at the University of Newcastle. He is author of *The Cult of Statistical Significance: How the Standard Error Costs Us Jobs, Justice, and Lives*.

HAIKU ECONOMICS

I'm an economist. Yet poetry is my first stop on the way to invention—discovery of metaphors. No matter the audience, a model is a metaphor. Not every economist understands that. Poetry can fill the gap between reason and emotion, adding feelings to economics. For example, Horace helps me relate to abstract mathematical theorists—colleagues I openly criticize—with "Gourmet à la Mode":

> It's not quite enough . . . to sweep up the fish
> From the most expensive fish stalls if you don't know which
> Go better with sauce and which, when served up broiled,
> Will make your jaded guest sit up and take notice.

I was teaching economics at the Georgia Institute of Technology when I made the haiku-economics connection. I needed to connect with 225 economics, science, and engineering majors—college kids who were being trained to believe that poetry and feelings are not important to, say, the World Bank. At the same time I was reading *The Essential Etheridge Knight* and falling in love with haiku. I thought about the inability of standard economic models to explain bubbles, crashes, and global inequality—and how market fundamentalists refuse to discuss them. I saw the bridge I needed in this poem:

> Invisible hand;
> Mother of inflated hope,
> Mistress of despair!

Adam Smith, indeed. Perhaps it's the economists who can learn the most from poets about precision and efficiency, about objectivity and maximization—the virtues, in other words, of value-free science.

Ironically, the benefit of the addition is in the cost. The typical haiku budget constraint is limited by three lines of seventeen syllables. Bashō himself understood well the joyful paradox of haiku economics: *less is more, and more is better!* Each poem is the length of about one human breath. This constraint, though severe, is more than offset by a boundless freedom to feel:

> Window reflection—
> The baby sparrow sitting,
> Listening to glass.

In his heartbreaking *Autobiography*, John Stuart Mill wrote about his inability to "feel" the economy. "I was in a dull state of nerves," Mill said. The great philosopher had been force-fed Jeremy Bentham's cost-benefit morality—so much so that the boy genius was dubbed "master" of political economy by age thirteen. At twenty he suffered a nervous breakdown, described at length in the same book. Passions and reason were systematically taught and cultivated by economists during the second half of the eighteenth century. But eventually Bentham's *Rationale of Reward* replaced Adam Smith's *Theory of Moral Sentiments*, and science thereby justified wholesale neglect of feeling. "From this neglect both in theory and in practice of the cultivation of feeling," Mill later concluded, "naturally resulted, among other things, an undervaluing of poetry, and of Imagination generally, as an element of human nature." His personal psychological battle against "hedonistic utilitarianism" and his subsequent breakdown could have been averted, he said, had he valued poetry: "I was wholly blind to its place in human culture, as a means of educating the feelings."

Nearly two centuries later, how's the old cultivation-of-feelings-and-imagination-in-economics project coming along? A snail's pace. "If you were to trace the separation of art from life historically," says the poet Etheridge Knight in an interview, "you would trace it back to the Greeks when Plato and others made the 'head thing' the ideal . . . There was a separation between reason and emotion." Like

Mill, Knight speaks from experience. Until he found poetry, "separation" was Knight's reality, too. "I died in Korea from a shrapnel wound," he says, "and narcotics resurrected me. I died in 1960 from a prison sentence, and poetry brought me back to life."

Plato's separation of art and life isn't science, you understand. Science favors Mill's, Knight's, and my belief that reason and emotion, speaking and feeling, are physically correlated variables. Speaking and feeling, like teaching and listening, are physical acts, governed by physical laws. "If it's true that as I'm talking to you bones are moving in your inner ears," Knight says, "I'm physically touching you with my voice." Images, sounds, and feelings are thus the original producers of I-to-We and cannot be separated. We cannot be separated. Yet in positive economics, it's all "value-free science."

"Generally speaking, a people's metaphors and figures of speech will come out of their basic economy," Knight continues. "If somebody lives near the ocean and they fish, their language will be full of those metaphors. If people are farmers, they will use that kind of figure of speech. Metaphors are alive. When they come into being, they are informed by the politics and the sociology and the economy of now. That's how language is."

That's how economic language is, too, but with a surprising difference. And this is where poets can help to fix the economy. It turns out that economic theory is overly dependent on fictional devices, whereas poetry, as Knight shows, trucks in the real.

Consider again the dominant metaphor of market economics: Adam Smith's "invisible hand." Proponents of the invisible-hand theory claim that free trade between rational self-interested people and nations leads—as if by an invisible hand—to higher wealth. Some take this to mean that collective attempts to steer economic outcomes (such as by giving welfare payments to the poor or by giving financial aid to foreign nations) will naturally backfire. People are already buying low and selling high, doing their best, the invisible talking hand says privately to economists. And the economy itself, here in the now, in 2011? Mother of inflated hope. Mistress of despair.

A professor of biology at the University of Utah, NALINI NADKARNI is the author of *Between Earth and Sky: Our Intimate Connections to Trees* and coeditor of *Forest Canopies* and *Monteverde: Ecology and Conservation of a Tropical Cloud Forest*.

GREEN I LOVE YOU GREEN

My work in this world is to understand forests through the approach of science. "Science" comes from the Latin *scio*: "to know as thoroughly as possible." When I visit my forest field sites in Costa Rica, I don mountain-climbing gear to ascend tall trees to study the rarely seen plants and animals that live high in the forest canopy. I then design experiments, gather data, and report quantitative findings to my scientific peers.

However, with the increasing environmental threats to forests caused by human activities—such as harvesting, fragmentation, and climate change—the definition of science must also include dissemination of information and extending a sense of mindfulness about trees to nonscientists. This communication must particularly include those who are unaware or only dimly aware of the importance of trees and nature, i.e., people who rarely visit a botanical garden or watch a nature documentary. To many of those people, the language and style of scientific communication are rarely compelling. What other vocabularies might scientists use to engage the public with the importance of nature and the enterprise of science?

"Poetry is prayer and good medicine," wrote a colleague of mine, Craig Carlson, when I asked for input on a book I was writing about the relationships between trees and humans. He was right. Consider Robert Morgan's "Translation," which is just one example of how a poem can capture a complex topic and integrate its rich meaning. Morgan describes the dance of organic matter from trunk to soil and back again to leaf. This poem parallels my own scientific papers, which explain the storage and transfers of nutrients in the endless and elegant circle of nutrient cycling:

Where trees grow thick and tall
In the original woods
The older ones are not
Allowed to fall but break

. . . .

To be absorbed by next
Of kin and feeding roots
Of soaring youth, to fade
Invisibly into
The shady floor in their
Translation to the future.

Poetry can make listeners aware of critical connections between humans and our biosphere. In the deceptively simple "inside out," Bill Yake reveals both the structural redundancy of form between human lungs and trees and their parallel function of gas exchange:

trees are our lungs turned inside out
& inhale our visible chilled breath.

our lungs are trees turned inside out
& inhale their clear exhalations.

Poems can also distill the compelling dualisms that exist in trees and in other parts of nature. For example, trees exemplify both strength and fragility. They both provide and require protection. Pam Galloway's poem "On Galiano" conveys their strength, and their inspiration of strength:

This tree stands
like a fork of lightning
shouting to me
of all that I could hold, look: the entire sky
if I would open up my arms, stretch
if I would let the air smooth my skin,
let it peel, knowing
there are stronger layers beneath.

But the fragility of trees must also be acknowledged. Scientific studies document that the tiny mandibles of a bark beetle can bring quick death to a jungle giant. A tropical fig tree species can go extinct if humans pump enough carbon dioxide into the atmosphere to raise the global temperature a single degree. Gail Mazur evokes this fragility in "Young Apple Tree, December":

> What you want for it you'd want
> for a child: that she take hold;
> that her roots find home in stony
>
> winter soil; that she take seasons
> in stride, seasons that shape and
> reshape her; that like a dancer's,
>
> her limbs grow pliant, graceful
> and surprising; that she know,
> in her branchings, to seek balance;
>
> that she know when to flower, when
> to wait for the returns; that she turn
> to a giving sun; that she know
>
> fruit as it ripens; that what's lost
> to her will be replaced; that early
> summer afternoons, a full blossoming
>
> tree, she cast lacy shadows; that change
> not frighten her.

Perhaps the deepest value of poetry for scientists is its articulation of the feelings that scientists themselves harbor for what they study—passion, deep curiosity, and a sense of stewardship. We would only rarely reveal these emotions to our scientific peers if we relied only upon the vocabulary of science. But poetry sets them free. "Verde que te quiero verde," as Federico García Lorca famously wrote, encapsulating the joy and the ultimate reason for my searchings. "Verde viento. Verdes ramas."

TRACEY JOHNSTONE is a midwife, poet, and author of legislation for the regulation of midwifery.

THE TRUE NATURE

I chose to leave the world of poetry to become a home-birth midwife as deliberately as Wendell Berry chose to be a farmer. A midwife's work is not simply to provide safe, evidence-based maternity care—it is to stitch together with families the emotions, physical sensations, and spiritual dynamics of birth into a meaningful whole. The vocation of midwife is my authentic answer to the call of being a poet.

Poetry was once my life. I was an editor with the university poetry magazine in my small southeastern city, and through luck and chutzpah the other editors and I connected with the Beat poets. Between 1991 and 1993 we brought Allen Ginsberg, Gregory Corso, Lawrence Ferlinghetti, and Diane di Prima to our city. We made all-nighter car trips to New York and read at St. Mark's and the Nuyorican Café. Thrust into this—suddenly, unexpectedly—was a baby. I was five months pregnant in March of 1991 when I watched the invasion of Kuwait on CNN. She roiled inside me with each televised mortar round and I felt the edges of myself dissolve between her body and the first of our TV wars:

> Everything is swinging: heaven, earth, water, fire,
> and the secret one slowly growing a body.
>
> Kabir

I had a long, challenging birth—unmedicated, hallucinatory, *poetic*. My room filled with every woman who has ever given birth or will give birth, witness to the last brutal and ecstatic efforts of my greatest poem—my daughter. My poetry changed. I delved even deeper into di Prima, Whitman, Rumi, Rilke, Rich, Berry; poets unaffected by the academic postmodern disdain of the "Grand Words"—Love, Revolution, Hope, Liberty, Peace, God, Beauty; words I was being warned off of in writing class because academia had decided they were tired, clichéd. Giving birth, becoming a mother with war in the background, made these words and the ideas behind them fierce, powerful, fresh. Real. I understood the office of the poet is to renew and actualize these words, not simply *describe*:

> You cannot write a single line w/out a cosmology
> a cosmogony
> laid out, before all eyes
>
> from "Rant," by Diane di Prima

In the fall of 1993 I attended the fifty-year Beat retrospective at NYU. I was elbowed out of the way by a celebrity because I was between her and a photographer. There were rock stars and movie stars. The words I had just become brave enough to reclaim—they crumbled under fashion and corporate cool. The following spring when Hunter S. Thompson came to my city, it was the antics of the famous actor traveling with him (preparing to play him in a movie) that were on the lips of the poetry girls. The binding on my Rilke broke that year:

> A god can do it. But will you tell me how
> A man can enter through the lyre's strings?
> Our mind is split. And at the shadowed crossing
> of heart-roads, there is no temple for Apollo.
> . . . .
> True singing is a different breath, about
> nothing. A gust inside the god. A wind.
>
> from *The Sonnets to Orpheus*

I slipped through the lyre strings of academic poetry and poetry of the New Cool. I slipped through them to birth, the truest song I had ever sung. I began a midwifery apprenticeship and learned to care for women and babies not only with skill and safety, but also in a way that honors the glorious relational sloppiness that involves time over efficiency, process over product. The families who choose to experience birth in all of its ecstasy, pain, effluvia, humor, and power, who reject the medical model of birth as illness, a condition to be treated, fundamentally understand that *we* are a creative process, the primary expression of a creative force. They are not afraid to be their own poets:

> What will I say
> to my fellow poets
> whose poems I do not read
> while this passion keeps me
> in the open?
>
> from *Clearing*, by Wendell Berry

A baby is born into the warm water of the birth tub. Her parents' hands raise her above the candle-licked surface. Unobtrusively I cup my hands under her head, supporting her above the water as she blinks a new world into focus. The first thing she sees—her mother and father kissing deeply over their creation, her being:

> No one lives in this room
> without confronting the whiteness of the wall
> behind the poems, planks of books,
> photographs of dead heroines.
> Without contemplating last and late
> the true nature of poetry. The drive
> to connect. The dream of a common language.
>
> from "Origins and History of Consciousness,"
> by Adrienne Rich

ALEX ROSS is the music critic of the *New Yorker*. His books include *The Rest Is Noise: Listening to the Twentieth Century* and the essay collection *Listen to This*.

THE IDEA OF ORDER

And the world was calm. It gives me a spell of peace to write these words, for the world is not calm. The sirens are louder than before. The helicopters ride low and rustle their black wings. The skinny white boys down the hall blast hip-hop against an intensifying psychic wind. Wallace Stevens's "The House Was Quiet and the World Was Calm" describes for me a state of visceral silence toward which my entire life is striving in vain: "The house was quiet because it had to be. / The quiet was part of the meaning, part of the mind: / The access of perfection to the page. / And the world was calm." What a world of nameless feeling rushes in before that "and." If I were reading the poem aloud, I would wait five long beats before going on. I hear an ambiguous chord, a half-diminished seventh in the horns and trombones, with tremolo strings all around. In that pause, the globe completes its turn toward midnight.

A beat-up paperback of *The Palm at the End of the Mind*—the Coop, $6.75—sits on my desk next to a German dictionary, a King James Bible, a Macintosh troubleshooting manual, and William James's *The Varieties of Religious Experience*. The book is both essential and practical; it helps me to live, it helps me to write. I've long believed that I write what I read, and Stevens is the magic well from which I draw. He teaches the implacable power of iambic meter, the heft of monosyllables, the democratic majesty of the English tongue. When I am at a loss, I open up the book and see what I can find—sometimes a word, sometimes a rhythm, sometimes just a reassurance. Perfection is possible. Reality gives way. It happened once, on a summer night in Connecticut.

Music must have something to do with it: I write about music, and Stevens is the most innately musical of poets. Composers have long felt a powerful attraction to him. Yet I know of no really successful Stevens songs. When John Adams set out to create a major choral work titled *Harmonium*, he naturally had Stevens in mind, but the poems were too proud to surrender to the encirclement of melody. Stevens is really a composer himself. Even the plainest words become chords of resonance, coalescing from hidden fundamentals. When *world* and *calm* materialize on the page, they thrum against each other like Messiaen's ecstatic triads.

There could never be an adequate setting of "The House Was Quiet and the World Was Calm," but there is one splendid parallel in the repertory. It appears in the first movement of Brahms's Fourth Symphony, when the lullingly simple first theme returns for the recapitulation. The melody is heard in broken form, its initial phrase slowed down and drawn out in a ghostly shimmer. Then comes a little pause, and the melody resumes in the middle of the phrase, as if no dark shape were staring through the window.

FERNANDO PEREZ played baseball professionally for ten years, most notably as an outfielder for the 2008 American League Champion Tampa Bay Rays. He is a youth mentor and teacher for the School of the New York Times and baseball analyst for MLB.tv. He writes a column at *Vice Sports* called "Recovering Ballplayer."

PARA RUMBIAR

I write from Caracas, the murder capital of the world, where I've been employed by the Leones to score runs and prevent balls from falling in the outfield. At the ankles of the Ávila Mountain among patches of dusky high-rises, the downtown grounds of el Estadio Universitario, packed beyond capacity, are ripe for a full-bodied poem. A mere pitching change is an occasion "para rumbiar," and the purse-lipped riot squad is always on the move with their spanking machetes swinging from their hips. The game isn't paced necessarily by innings or score. It's marked by the pulsating bass drums of the samba band that trail bright, scantily clad, headdressed goddesses strutting about the mezzanine. The young fireworks crew stands mere feet from flares that don't always set out vertically, sometimes landing in the outfield still aflame. "The wave" includes heaving drinks into the sky.

In earning my stripes as a professional baseball player I've been through many cities and have stared out of hotel windows all over the Americas. Ball players are mercenaries, taking assignments indiscriminately. Throughout the minor leagues you'll find yourself slouched on a bus, watching small towns roll by matter-of-factly like stock-market tickers, on your back in a new nondescript room, or "shopping for images" (Allen Ginsberg) in a Wal-Mart, hunched over a cart in no rush.

Like poetry, baseball is a kind of counterculture. The (optional) isolation from the outside world (which I often opt for), the idleness about which—and out of which—so many poems are written or sung: I see this state of mind as a blessing. Sometimes, in fact, when I haven't turned on a television or touched a newspaper for months, freed from the corporate bombast, poetry is the only dialect I recognize.

Long ago Robert Creeley confirmed my suspicion that words strung even sparingly together can be as aurally powerful as anything else we have. He has been my most important poet, because I can take him anywhere, like oranges—even reduced to nothing in both physical and mental exhaustion, nauseous and half asleep bussing from a red-eye.

One of my first managers always preached separation from the game for the sake of our own health, and for the sake of our performance. The game can be maddening, and we ought to corner ourselves in this trade only so far. I'm in love with baseball, but eventually my prime will end, and she'll slowly break my heart. Baseball has remained remarkably impervious to modernity, but is, like any modern industry, highly alienating. I turn to poetry because it is less susceptible to circumstance. I'm not especially touched when a poet deals with a ball game; I'm not especially interested in having one world endear itself to the other. Right now I need them apart, right now I'm after displacement, contrast. The thick wilderness of, say, late Ashbery can wrangle with the narrowness of competition.

Cellist NICHOLAS PHOTINOS is a founding member of the Grammy Award–winning music ensemble Eighth Blackbird. He has performed and recorded with artists including Björk and Wilco, and jazz artists such as violinist Zach Brock and singer Grazyna Auguscik.

LUCID, INESCAPABLE RHYTHMS

I am the cellist in a chamber music group called Eighth Blackbird, which was titled as a reference to American poet Wallace Stevens's "Thirteen Ways of Looking at a Blackbird," the eighth stanza of which reads:

> I know noble accents
> And lucid, inescapable rhythms;
> But I know, too,
> That the blackbird is involved
> In what I know.

When you call your group Eighth Blackbird, you have to expect that people will ask questions, and we've been explaining our name—happily—for over a decade. Sometimes we'll give a full-blown account of how our violinist, who was studying early twentieth-century American poetry, came up with the name, and how we briefly considered "red wheelbarrow," another classic. Often, though, we'll just give a short explanation and finish reading the stanza, to leave the questioner thinking about what those words might mean.

What do they mean to us? The first few words resound with great power. Noble accents, lucid, inescapable rhythms: these are the things we strive to create each day in rehearsal and onstage. And yet there is that hidden element—the blackbird—that lies beneath everything. What is the blackbird, and how is the blackbird involved? An enigma, and rightfully so, since I believe there should be an element of the unknown to art, something that leaves you thinking, that makes you ask questions. It is that element that sums up why we named ourselves Eighth Blackbird: we wanted people to ask why, and it is a fantastic thing to be able to leave them with some great poetry in reply.

Poetry in music is a tricky thing; whether spoken or sung, it is a common reaction among audiences and musicians alike to want the words to be in the foreground, and I know of at least one well-known composer who is reluctant to set text in music lest the music take a backseat to the words. Poetry in music will often determine nearly every element in a musical composition, including length, structure, rhythm, orchestration, harmony, mood, and style, and requires that the musical interpreter have a solid understanding of the poetry in order to give a convincing performance. Often this is a good thing, and the composer intends that the performer look to the poetry for guidance and a deepening of interpretation. But some composers have fought this; in Arnold Schoenberg's famous *Pierrot Lunaire*, the text of which is the German translation of twenty-one short poems by Albert Giraud, the composer's foreword to the performers states:

> The performers' task here is at no time to derive the mood and character of the individual pieces from the meaning of the words, but always solely from the music. To the extent that the tone-painterly representation of the events and feelings in the text were of importance to the composer, it will be found in the music anyway. Wherever the performer fails to find it, he must resist adding something that the composer did not intend. If he did so, he would not be adding, but subtracting.

This is perhaps an understandable sentiment coming from a composer and is essentially no different from the screenwriter admonishing an actor to stick to the script when the actor starts improvising. However, it seems superfluous in several ways: while Schoenberg is right that much of the poetry is represented in the music, it would seem odd to ignore a major component of the work—the poetry—in constructing an artistic interpretation of the piece. Instructing the performer to rely on what is to be "found in the music anyway" is a bit haphazard, for every musician will find different things. What decent musician, one who is really dedicated to understanding and performing this amazing work, would not want to come to know the poetry behind it all? And once knowing, how could it fail to influence his interpretation?

These issues arise even in music that is seemingly without words. When I was first learning Ernest Bloch's work for cello and orchestra *Schelomo*, I was wrapped up in the pure sensuality of the piece without really knowing anything about its namesake, King Solomon. My teacher told me to read the passage of Ecclesiastes 1:2–9, which is the inspiration for *Schelomo*. The passage begins with the famous line "Vanity of vanities, all is vanity," and ends in despair:

> All things toil to weariness:
> Man cannot utter it.
> The eye is not satisfied with seeing,
> Nor the ear filled with hearing.
> That which hath been
> Is that which shall be,
> And that which hath been done
> Is that which shall be done;
> And there is nothing new under the sun.

This was not the Solomon of the Song of Songs—robust, full of life and love—but Solomon at the end of his days, still powerful but world-weary. This dramatically changed how I viewed and played the piece, and in concrete ways: the addition of a slower, wearier vibrato; a sense of struggle in much of the middle passages, recalling former glory; and toward the end a sense of exhaustion, of almost not making it to the next note, until finally ending in complete negation.

ALFRED MOLINA is an English American actor, known for his roles in *Raiders of the Lost Ark*, *Maverick*, *Spider-Man 2*, *Chocolat*, *The Da Vinci Code*, *An Education*, *Rango*, and *Prince of Persia: The Sands of Time*.

"TWO LOVES I HAVE . . ."

Like many adolescent boys with few physical skills, I found reading a refuge as much as a requirement while I was at school. It sparked a love of words, and a love of performing, that have never deserted me. I recognized, even at that early age, the storytelling power of poetry. Reading verse out loud became a lifelong pleasure and inspiration. I was introduced to Robert Browning, Kipling, and Wordsworth. Browning in particular provided plenty of imagery and characterization for an aspiring actor to grapple with. "My Last Duchess," for example, with its precision in describing the dramatic moment, the tension between the participants as well as the art on display, created a scene that lived in my mind as clearly as a shot from a movie. It was all there, everything I needed to know about the speaker and his attitude towards his faithless mistress. "I gave commands; / Then all smiles stopped together. There she stands / As if alive." The poem reads like a deliciously full and revealing soliloquy from a character revealing his anger and sense of betrayal at every turn.

I soon discovered that poetry provides a laboratory for actors. Shakespeare's sonnets, perfectly proportioned observations, were like little self-contained dramas. The speaker presents a dilemma or an emotional state, describes the effect it is having, and resolves the argument by either accepting or refusing what fate offers. It seemed to me each sonnet was a microcosm of everything I might be likely to experience in my life. Youthful love, bitter disappointment, cynical acceptance, advancing age and decrepitude, and finally the shadow of death itself were all to be found within the boundary of three quatrains and a couplet. This was more than just poetry, more than literature. This was theater, spoken by characters living in a dramatic moment made real by the depth of their feeling and experience. I began to "act" them for myself. As I got older and began to study verse more seriously, it was clear that these poems could reveal character, motivation, and "backstory," all the things that actors agonize over as we try to analyze and embody the character we play. Of course, Shakespeare was a playwright, so it may seem self-evident that his sonnets would be theatrical, but other poets who were not playwrights had the same effect on me, and I still read them as a way to find the voice of a character.

Over time, reading poems became a habit. I was always drawn toward rhymed verse because of the rhythms, and the regularity of the meter suited my nonintellectual approach. But as I gained confidence, I began to explore the more complex structures of poets like Gerard Manley Hopkins and, later, the Beats. I was attracted to anything that sounded like a "character" talking. Poetry became linked in my mind with performance, a notion most poets would cringe at, I fancy. I suppose this is a very unliterary view of literature. In the bloom of my youth and ignorance, that link I forged between poetry and the physical muscularity of performance was always reinforced when I heard poets read poetry. They seemed to be seeking objectivity, using a certain vocal tone that left the field of interpretation clear of any nuance. They struck me as dull and uninviting, rather like opera singers trying to swing. It was a dry experience just when I was thirsty for fire and guts. In recent times, the work of rappers and the exposure of rap poets on TV shows like *Def Poetry Jam* have resuscitated that link for me.

The act of speaking is physical, full of breath and energy. Combine that with a great poem, and the words can become powerful, momentous, and capable of shifting our perceptions and challenging our view of the world.

I was born from the poetic lives my parents
lived and was raised in a tragic city.

RHYMEFEST

Do we disqualify one because he rhymes over a
breakbeat instead of a lyre? Because one is blind
while the other is merely def?

ROB KENNER

Scottish singer-songwriter MOMUS (Nick Currie) has published books of speculative fiction and appeared as a performance artist, offering "unreliable tours" and "emotional lectures."

WRITTEN IN ROCK CANDY

I love the artistic use of short bursts of language. Give them a name and a role, though—*poetry*, for instance—and you risk rebuilding some of the things that their freshening surprise can, one hopes, undermine: guilds, codes of conduct, etiquettes, habits.

Language can be sclerotic: a boring, repetitive, normative, legitimizing thing, a descriptive system with prescriptive and proscriptive aspirations. But language is at its most charming when it abandons the will to power and substitutes pure play. A lyric Paddy McAloon levered into an early Prefab Sprout song springs to mind:

> Words are trains for moving past
> what really has no name.
>
> from "Couldn't Bear to Be Special"

If that were poetry in the most limited definition, it would be mere words on a page. But the way I remember it, the elegant phrase is hollered out, slowly yet violently, on a vinyl record. It sounds like an existential cry of pain, but there's a giddy sense of freedom edging through. The irreducible otherness of things has a fierce beauty that language can never capture. And maybe language can be a beautiful thing-in-itself too.

There's poetry in my family: both my great-grandfather and his father won the bardic crown at the Hebridean festival known as the Mod. As a child I played with the silver laurel crown, draping my head with its ripped blue velvet covering. Sadly, as a non-Gaelic speaker, I can't read their poems. One, I'm told, is about the steamer my great-grandfather piloted up and down the Clyde. He must've scribbled his verses on the bridge. In that sense, he wasn't a professional poet, even if the crown conferred the qualification of "bard."

Writing lyrics for songs, I feel as if I'm continuing an amateur tradition in which words are just one element in a whirling and impure confluence, a confection of many media. Here, words only come alive when animated by a specific voice, and instruments, and visuals.

When I was first impressed by glam rock figures like Marc Bolan and David Bowie, it was partly their physical beauty that snared me: they had an obviously charismatic sexual grace, a way of dressing and of moving that appealed enormously. But they also used words in an intriguing way: over atonal stride note clusters, Bowie would sing elegiac cabaret songs ("Sake and strange divine / You'll make it") while Bolan would write fairytale doggerel ("Light all the fires, it's the king of the rumbling spires!")

In retrospect, such stuff was the next logical step from childhood pantomime and the poems my mother would read me—cautionary or lunatic tales by Hilaire Belloc and Edward Lear concerning Matilda or "The Dong with a Luminous Nose."

When I was twelve I heard two pieces of poetry set to music that absolutely boggled my mind. One was "Façade" by Edith Sitwell, with jazz-age music by William Walton. Mr. Head, my music teacher, sat us down in a dingy classroom and played the whole thing on an enormous wooden record player. I particularly liked the lugubrious passages:

> Cried the navy-blue ghost
> Of Mr. Belaker
> The allegro negro cocktail-shaker:
> "Why did the cock crow,
> Why am I lost
> Down the endless road to Infinity toss'd?"

The music—a spectral waltz—was absolutely integral to my experience. It meshed perfectly with Bowie's pantomimic readings of Evelyn Waugh's *Decline and Fall.*

The other revelation was hearing a brass ensemble accompanying a reading of Eliot's "Prufrock." One of the housemasters at my boarding school had written it. The injection of evocative words into a colorfield of sound was exactly what I loved about the music of Bolan and Bowie, but Eliot's lines mingled the known and the unknown much better, melding a universal melancholia with glimpses of privileged and exotic interiors:

> I have measured out my life with coffee spoons;
> I know the voices dying with a dying fall
> Beneath the music from a farther room.

Soon I would be written through like rock candy by the phrases of poets. Poems didn't just supply musical phrases, but narrative tricks that other media couldn't. Robert Browning's "My Last Duchess," for instance, demonstrated that a poem could be a dramatic, icy-spined monologue with an unreliable narrator:

> I gave commands;
> Then all smiles stopped together. There she stands
> As if alive. Will't please you rise?

And Rilke's *Duino Elegies*, which seductively suggest that perhaps we (poets? or human beings in general?) are only here "for saying: house, bridge, fountain, gate, jug, fruit-tree, window—at most: column, tower . . . but for saying, realize, oh, for a saying such as the things themselves would never have profoundly said!" (translated by J. B. Leishman and Stephen Spender).

But Rilke—with his conflation of poets and humans, and his celebration of an apparently sacred duty to name the nameless—strays perhaps too far into the hubris of professional poetry. Today I might draw just as much verbal pleasure from a Tumblr feed called *Curatorial Poetry*, which presents "found poems" from the pages of art catalogs:

> Very exotic foliage, resembling palm trees, with oversize
> parrots and dragonflies. The upper portion of the box
> contains a pattern of white stars. Printed in pink and
> varnished green on a yellow ground. Very faded.

That's all I need, and my brain races.

WILL OLDHAM is a singer-songwriter and actor, better known as Bonnie "Prince" Billy. He has collaborated with many artists, including the Cairo Gang, Dawn McCarthy, Mike Aho, and Trembling Bells.

TO HELL WITH DRAWERS

The difference between lyrics and poetry is that I don't understand poetry. I don't understand biology either. Someone must be there to guide me through the meanings of things. Lyrics, recorded and sung, have the opportunity to sink long and thoroughly; they can work on and with the subconscious. We have long ago passed the time when poetry is memorized without such aid, and sitting there on the paper a poem makes me feel ignorant and insane.

Even recited, words expressively coded and adjacented are like a miracle of phonetics but do not mean what they should. It's about the structure, but a poem holds nothing up and nothing in. It sits there. And in a public space, a read poem fills the air with signs that I cannot use to direct myself anywhere except the restroom or the sidewalk, or inside of myself.

Recently I read a review of *Shame*, a movie "about" sex addiction, and the reviewer boldly and awkwardly quoted a Shakespeare sonnet in order to say something about lust: "All this the world well knows; yet none knows well / To shun the heaven that leads men to this hell." It made complete sense to me and got me searching for the full sonnet. Unfortunately, the full sonnet made no sense to me, and even that quoted couplet became scrambled and indecipherable without the guidance of a critic to give it meaning—because it is poetry, and poetry is something that points to something else.

I also do not like drawers. There must be shelves, where the contents are visible. When things are hidden in drawers, they do not exist. Doors must be open. Prose is shelving. On lust, Iris Murdoch (about whom I know nothing except that her writing is mocked in a weird British movie I vaguely recall seeing) wrote: "The absolute yearning of one human body for another particular one and its indifference to substitutes is one of life's major mysteries." And that is a shelf with its contents quite viewable. It's like: Yes. Whereas the versed lines of the bard are more like: Ouch.

Coding is fine, but mostly when given a clue or some other assistance to its solution. This can be done by setting the words to music and then singing them. Leonard Cohen sings, "I needed so much / To have nothing to touch / I've always been greedy that way." I have heard that line so many times in my head that it functions like propaganda. It has become a part of my lang-scape. Take Cohen's book *Death of a Lady's Man*, in which each piece is juxtaposed with a counterpoint to shed light on both. I can read that shit. I can read most verse, but it dissipates so quickly because my stupid modern mind travels so fast to another place that the lines are gone.

Give me a melody—give me, better, a harmonized melody—and those words will become a part of me. This is what I, a child of the age, need. I'm ready for a return to epic balladry when it all comes grumbling down and we must actually use these memory cells we've been given. I am always crying inside to have things integrate and interrelate, but having grown up having to find and appreciate things on my own, and on my own terms, it now takes a grander force to pierce the defenses and get the party started in my soul than it may for many others. My mind isn't a sponge, it's a parasitic death-starry glob that is big and wet and angry much of the time, feeding on itself and allowing only the choicest and most-vulnerable bits in when its blood sugar gets low. It longs for a projectile to penetrate and obliterate its oneness and let the stockpile plenish billions.

At least that's what it feels like sometimes. My mind is kept in a drawer, in the end. And the drawer hides its contents from view, like a poem. So really, poems and cabinets only make me hurt because I resent those who love them.

RHYMEFEST (Che Smith) is a writer, artist, activist, political organizer, and teacher. His many awards include a Grammy, Golden Globe, and an Academy Award. He cofounded Donda's House in 2013 with Kanye West and Donnie Smith.

MY LIFE IS A POEM

Chicago is a poem written by Edgar Allan Poe. It is beautifully tragic, with its political corruption, murder, suspense, segregation, and economic disparity. "Deep into that darkness peering, long I stood there wondering, fearing, / Doubting, dreaming dreams no mortal ever dared to dream before." All the while, creating from within it are many of the most prolific artists, athletes, and world figures humanity has ever encountered.

My mother was a poem written by Gwendolyn Brooks. Fifteen years old from Chicago with a baby of her own to raise, she was simple but profound. Strong in spirit yet subtle in approach.

> Young, and so thin, and so straight.
> So straight! as if nothing could ever bend her.
> But poor men would bend her, and doing things with
>   poor men,
> . . . .
> And the rest of things in life that were for poor women.
>
> from "Jessie Mitchell's Mother"

She was searching for love in a world of rejection. She found her gifts through the wisdom that only age, experience, and letting go of the past could bring.

My father is a poem written by Maya Angelou. He is a character that is harsh if you have a one-dimensional view of the world, but gorgeous through the lens of a dynamic soul.

> How to find my soul a home
> Where water is not thirsty

And bread loaf is not stone
I came up with one thing
And I don't believe I'm wrong
That nobody,
But nobody
Can make it out here alone.

from "Alone"

He was abused by his father, he abused alcohol, he abandoned his only child and walked a twenty-eight-year journey through homelessness, yet he has kept a healthy sense of humor and aspires to more. This stands as a testament to his good nature.

I am a poem written by hip-hop. I was born from the poetic lives my parents lived and was raised in a tragic city. My story unfolds under the crumbling infrastructure of Chicago's South Side. I saw words everywhere and my attraction to them was magnetic.

Hands to the Heavens, no man no weapon,
Formed against, yes Glory is destined.
Everyday women and men become Legends,
Sins that go against our skin become blessings.

from "Glory"

As a young man I tried to process every word I came across: colorful graffiti written on walls, trains, and buses, placed in strategic positions for all to see. Dilapidated billboards and signs sat above mom-and-pop stores that seemed to oddly make their businesses more familiar and welcoming. I listened to the rhythm of conversations, realizing as a child that words and rhythms are two separate entities that work in tandem to create beauty.

In fact, I never called what I'd absorbed as a youth poetry; in my neighborhood it was called hip-hop. It was a culture of youth expressing our frustrations, showing our gifts and celebrating life through break dance (b-boying), music (DJing), visual art (graffiti), community (knowledge), and my favorite element, rap.

Rapping became an avenue to vent my anger as a teenager without resorting to violence; it was an acceptable means to show the world my affinity for words; it was a positive way to gain attention and perhaps even a career path. Through my elementary and high school years I was a mystery to my teachers. I never turned in any assignments and made failing grades even though they always saw me writing in class. They would tell my mother, "We see him doing the work, he just never hands it in." The only thing I was working on were raps, perfecting the organization of words. I was memorizing long verses, learning to write in my head without using pen and paper. To this day I write music in my head, then transcribe it after its completion.

I ended up dropping out of high school and I never completed college. The only thing that I've been consistent with is words. I've lived by the belief that we should choose our enemies wisely, instead of our battles. For in an enemy, all battles can be predicted. My enemy was, and continues to be, miseducation.

Words have lead me to a Critics' Choice Award, Grammy, Golden Globe, and Academy Award for cowriting songs like "Jesus Walks" and "Glory." Words have blessed me with a career. Words are my superpower. I use them to heal, I use them to build. My words have led me back to Chicago to help create a program called Donda's House. I teach gifted young people who possess the same dedication to words. I want them to connect their hip-hop to the world's poetry.

Words can create worlds, and I've discovered that poetry can be not only read but also lived out.

My life is a poem.

JOLIE HOLLAND is an American songwriter, bandleader, multi-instrumentalist, singer, performer, poet, and author.

LOOSENING THE GRIP

No, I don't read much poetry these days. There's just no need for it, because I get enough through my ears, and from the mess that's already reverberating around my skull.

When I was thirteen, I used to get high on Dylan Thomas, Blake, Wilde, and Yeats. And I wrote poetry incessantly. It was a personal meditation that had very little to do with anything that went on at school. I was entranced by form, motif, and repetition. It makes sense that I became a songwriter.

As a teenager, I remember reading somewhere that *The Ballad of Reading Gaol* by Oscar Wilde was considered one of the most perfectly constructed poems in the English language. (Of course it was Morrissey and The Smiths that led me to read Wilde in the first place—their song "Cemetry Gates" refers to him.) The idea of perfect structure and execution fascinated me, and how structure in songs is tempered and tried by lyrical rhythm—that is to say, how well it can be said out loud or in your head.

My friend Brian Miller wrote a whole album's worth of music to Yeats's poems, called *Yeats Is Greats*. I covered one of those songs, "Wandering Angus," on my first album, *Catalpa*. Those well-constructed English ballads held up perfectly to the necessities of the music. They had more flow and balance than a lot of the lyrics that are designed as such.

But like I was saying about getting it through the ears, I want to tell you that this very instant, as I have set myself down at the corner bar to have dinner and write in my journal, I hear these words from a seventies Jamaican recording coming in over the speakers:

There is a land far far away
Where there's no night, there's only day.
Look into the Book of Life and you will see—
That there's a land far far away.

from "Statta Massagana," by the Abyssinians

Through my experience of this Rastafarian chorus, I remember Emily Dickinson's very useful definition of poetry: that which makes one feel as though the top of one's head has been taken off. I feel exactly what she was describing. To be very clear, the sensation is like having an acupuncture needle placed at one's crown point, at the top of one's head. That same sort of physical cue is exactly the kind of meter I check when I'm deciding about music. My friend Tim Freeman in Texas says, "You can tell whether it's good music or bad depending on whether it loosens or tightens 'the grip of obscure emotions.'"

Just as dinosaurs didn't really disappear but became birds, poems have become songs. I have no interest in bemoaning the fact that the poetry most widely consumed these days is oral: the roots of our poetic literature are in Homer, who chanted or sang his words.

I remember how one especially ignorant (white) critic of Zora Neale Hurston complained that a sermon she'd written into one of her books was too fanciful to have come out of the mouth of an "uneducated" black preacher. But our Zora, a pioneer anthropologist, had recorded and quoted said sermon verbatim. Let us not forget she was present and influential at many of the great recording sessions that Alan Lomax conducted. The Lomax recordings of the Georgia Sea Island Singers contain, to me, some of the most important American poems:

Adam in the garden
Picking up leaves
God called Adam
Picking up leaves
Adam wouldn't answer
Picking up leaves
God called Adam
Picking up leaves

"Adam!"
Picking up leaves
Adam wouldn't answer
"Adam! Where art thou?"
Called, "I'm ashamed"
God called Adam
Adam wouldn't answer

The group stomps and claps while they chant "picking up leaves," and the leader, in a strong voice, calls out the alternating words. This is a beautiful group meditation on the mythic material, which describes the first moments a human being ever felt shame. If we can imagine the first moment a person experienced shame, we are given the opportunity to imagine a psychological space that existed before shame. It is a profoundly restorative and useful meditation, improvised within a community that could shelter and amplify one's experience. This song, these words (without musical accompaniment), are some of the flowers of American oral culture.

I believe I am so moved by a good gospel song partly because it tends to the experiential. I know that song is designed to be of use, to move people, to move one's energy. Like Emily said, to take the top of your head off. Words on the page that can do that for me are few and far between. Songs that have that power are likewise few. A lot of songs and poetry are emanations of souls that have no power of internal motion, and therefore can provide no inspiration for anyone else. Certainly, a lot of people are interested in music and poetry that doesn't crack open the top of their heads. But I don't have room here to discuss why terrible music and poetry have been popular.

I don't know how to talk about what poetry is, except to talk about the experience. It's good to have your hand on the rudder and know when the current is moving powerfully. One thing I've enjoyed noticing is that both classical Zen haiku and my favorite American music have at least one little trick in common. I'd describe the way that classic Zen haiku works in this way: the poet describes the world, and describes his own mind, in one deft and beautiful stroke. It's like a report of what's in front of and behind the eyes. Here are a couple of sweet Bashō poems that do this:

temple bell
also sounds like it is
cicada's voice

. . .

On a journey,
Resting beneath the cherry blossoms,
I feel myself to be in a Noh play.

And now check out how this verse by Gram Parsons works:

We flew straight across that river bridge
last night half past two.
Switchman waved his lantern "goodbye and good day"
as we went rolling through.
Billboards and truck stops pass by the grievous angel,
Now I know just what I have to do.

from "Return of the Grievous Angel"

I love how that last line comes out of nowhere. It is so direct and big-souled.

ROB KENNER is a music journalist living in New York City. He is the founder and publisher of Boomshots.com and author of a forthcoming history of reggae music's worldwide impact.

WORD'S WORTH

For better or worse, poetry has always been as familiar as breathing to my six siblings and me. As the offspring of a loving, lifelong literary critic, Hugh Kenner, we were used to spontaneous recitations. Stray refrigerator magnet nouns and verbs would mix up with our breakfast cereal. Headlines from the daily news became haikus or, worse, free verse. I considered it perfectly normal to telephone Louis Zukofsky to discuss "similes" for a sixth-grade homework assignment. My sister Lisa once served Basil Bunting's sake, keeping his goblet filled as he read during a Pound conference. In the house where we grew up, a framed William Carlos Williams typescript, signed with his painful post-stroke scrawl, hung where you could examine it while taking a leak.

Of course we watched plenty of Bugs Bunny and Road Runner cartoons. But at bedtime, while other kids might be hearing Christopher Robin's observations on the changing of the guard at Buckingham Palace, my father and I would learn poems from books that I've chosen to hide from my own kids for the time being. *The Bad Child's Book of Beasts* and *More Beasts for Worse Children* were two of our favorites. These were the work of Hilaire Belloc, an early-twentieth-century British poet whose verse was "designed for the admonition of children between the ages of eight and fourteen years." By the time I was seven I could spit out the whole grisly tale of "Jim," a boy who runs away at the zoo and gets eaten by Ponto the lion:

> Now just imagine how it feels
> When first your toes and then your heels
> And then by gradual degrees
> Your shins and ankles, calves and knees

Are slowly eaten bit by bit.
No wonder Jim detested it!

Come to think of it, maybe it wasn't such a leap for me to end up at *VIBE* magazine. Back when Lisa introduced me to LL Cool J and Kool Moe Dee, we never doubted that rap was poetry; we had always understood poems to be performances. Although lots of mindless, hurtful crap gets peddled by the corporate entertainment machine, the essence of rap is *samizdat* poetry.

It's an essential part of being human, this need to shape the chaos of life into language and then to fit that mosaic of words into rhythmic patterns. At the end of the day, Nas and Homer are both in the same line of work. Do we disqualify one because he rhymes over a breakbeat instead of a lyre? Because one is blind while the other is merely def?

Our father taught my siblings and me that a work of art should reward prolonged attention, a test that the best hip-hop passes with ease. These compositions operate on several levels at once: you can dance to the beat, let the verbal flow wash over you, or wear out your rewind button trying to penetrate the encrypted language. With the best MCs (as most serious rappers prefer to be called) there is no lack of hidden riches. Where Milton may shout out Dante and the Book of Revelation, Jay-Z alludes to The Notorious B.I.G. and Big Daddy Kane, all while taunting rival rappers, social critics, and law enforcement officials. In "Agent Orange" Pharoahe Monch pisses on the White House lawn, then lets the double entendres fly:

I threw a rock and I ran . . . Y'all wanna ask me who sane?
These biological gases are eating my brain
It's a political grab bag to rape mother earth
Thirty seconds after they bagged dad for what he's worth.

I once had the good fortune to edit Harry Allen's "Hypertext," an attempt to unpack all the embedded subliminal references and nuances of craftsmanship in "Niggas Bleed," a single rap by the late Christopher Wallace, aka The Notorious B.I.G. The final manuscript—fragments of which appeared in the March 1998 issue of *VIBE*—ran way past twenty thousand words. The complexity of

Wallace's rap was awe-inspiring, especially considering the fact that he wrote nothing down, recording all his rhymes "off the dome."

Meanwhile, millions of kids around the world can recite Eminem's latest verse by heart, although they couldn't care less what any doctoral candidate thinks about it. "See I'm a poet to some / A regular modern day Shakespeare," Eminem muses on "Renegade," a dazzling duet from Jay-Z's landmark album *The Blueprint*. Because it's not exactly cool for any MC to care about that sort of thing—let alone a white boy—he backpedals a few lines later: "I'm just a kid from the gutter / Making this butter offa these bloodsuckers." But go through his raps and Eminem's artistic aspirations are undeniable. Tupac Shakur, hip-hop's tragic antihero, struggled with a similar internal conflict. Only after his murder at age twenty-five did his legions of fans learn how much he loved acting classes and writing poetry.

Mercenary motives are reliable alibis for the preservation of icy machismo. ("Words worth a million like I'm rapping over platinum teeth," Jay-Z once boasted.) But other MCs are willing to admit that it's not necessarily all about the Benjamins. Check Common's new album *Be*, especially "The Corner," an ode to the urban crossroads that features the seventies proto-rap crew The Last Poets. Some MCs actually covet critical respect. "I'm trying to show these poetry niggas that you can be poetic and into high fashion at the same time," the Chicago-born bard Kanye West told *VIBE*. "These people think you need to live on a rock to be poetic. I'm actually consulting with poets as I write this album. Like the way niggas got vocal coaches, I got a poetry coach."

Reports of the declining state of poetry have been greatly exaggerated. Much of the mail we receive at *VIBE* (especially the letters stamped with a prison ID) contains loose-leaf sheets of handwritten poetry. Is this what the poet Allen Grossman had in mind when he called poetry "the last recourse before despair"? Or what Lucille Clifton was getting at when she wrote:

> . . . come celebrate
> with me that everyday
> something has tried to kill me
> and has failed.

Hugh Kenner was no hip-hop head. His auditory sense was severely compromised for most of his life, and those powerful hearing aids of his would have made listening to one of my favorite mix-tapes a painful experience. As far as I know, his only exposure to rap lyrics came while watching the first annual *VIBE* Awards on TV with the closed captions turned on. Mom and Lisa sat with him as Andre 3000 enjoined the crowd to "shake it like a Polaroid picture." Dad expressed his sympathy that I had to attend this event and then died four days later of heart failure. But I still believe that he'd fully endorse my defense of the ol' boom-bap. After all, consider his epitaph: "What thou lov'st well remains. The rest is dross."

NEKO CASE is a singer and songwriter who performs solo under her own name and with the Canadian-bred rock band The New Pornographers. Her most recent album is *case/lang/veirs*.

MY FLAMING HAMSTER WHEEL OF PANIC ABOUT PUBLICLY DISCUSSING POETRY IN THIS RESPECTED FORUM

When I was asked by *Poetry* to write an article for them I was ecstatic. I was flattered. I felt important! I agreed immediately. About twenty minutes after sending my e-mail of acceptance I paused to triumphantly sharpen my claws on the bookcase when I noticed the blazing, neon writing on the wall. It said: YOU'VE NEVER EVEN PASSED ENGLISH 101 AND EVERYONE WHO READS THIS MAGAZINE WILL KNOW IT. Why do I care? I'm not sure. I think it's because I don't want to let poetry down. Poetry is such a delicate, pretty lady with a candy exoskeleton on the outside of her crepe-paper dress. I am an awkward, heavy-handed mule of a high school dropout. I guess I just need permission to be in the same room with poetry.

I think the fear began in about fifth grade. Right off the top they said poetry was supposed to have "form." Even writing a tiny haiku became a wrestling match with a Claymation Cyclops for me. (I watched a lot of *Sinbad*.) We aren't too cool for poetry; it's the other way around. At least that's the impression I took from public school. The fact that these feelings would remain into adulthood is ridiculous. We all have the right to poetry! How could I still think it's for other people? Smarter people. What's doubly confusing is I don't have the same reservations when poetry is accompanied by music. Perhaps I feel that way because there is music all around us—it's the wallpaper of our lives. It's not considered precious in American culture unless a symphony is performing it.

I *do* know when a string of printed words busts my little dam and the tears spill over and I sponge them up with my T-shirt. I couldn't give you that formula before it happens, it just hits me like a bat to the face. That's a sweet, hot, amazing, embarrassing moment. It even makes me feel a little included, as if I have to be "ready for the poetry" for it to be happening.

I can't choose which kind of poetry I like best. Sonnets? Prose? I don't know the terminology. I just blurt out some fragmented gibberish into the vast, woodsy country of poetry. It freezes in midair. Here come some examples now . . .

Shakespeare's *Titus Andronicus* haunts me. Aaron's death speech is veiled, venomous gospel music. I read it over and over even though I've already memorized it like a teenage girl in love. W. H. Auden scares me under the couch (even when he's being funny). I hold my flashlight on "The Witnesses," with its haunting "humpbacked surgeons / And the scissors man," until my arm shakes, my trusty dictionary in my other hand. Dorothy Parker makes me manic! I can't even make it through the first three lines of "The Godmother" without bursting into tears. Lynda Barry and Sherman Alexie save my life constantly. They battle identity crises with a sense of humor and a language that speaks so hard to me because they came from my home, in my own time, and they talk to me in our special parlance. They tell me I'm not crazy because they remember it too. It really is the old Washington State that created my personal brain-picture ABCs. (D is for "Douglas fir.") The same Washington State I can never go back to. Barry and Alexie volunteer to go in my place. Their memories make friends with mine. I can't live without them.

What do these poets have in common? They don't write sycophantic, roman-numeral-volumed postcards to God. They don't get all "love-ity-love-love" either. I get the sense they imagine their audience and want to comfort them. They are so good at it they even have the ability to comfort us with scariness. Sadness too. I think that is a powerful magic. They don't just write poetry either; they are playwrights and painters and singers and novelists.

How can we help them out? I guess we keep on needing them, even if it's kind of a secret. If the poets handed out anonymous comment cards for us shy poetry lovers to fill out so they could get a better idea of what we needed, I would direct them to the Osborne

Brothers' bluegrass classic "Rocky Top." They say in two lines what poets and writers "Anna Karenina" themselves to death to convey, about a girl who's "wild as a mink, but sweet as soda pop / I still dream about that." If those lines were written about me I could lie down and die. It is perfection. Uncool Perfection.

Singer SALLY TIMMS was born in Leeds, England, and grew up in the Yorkshire Dales. In 1985 she joined the band Mekons as a full-time member and has regretted it ever since.

POETRY OUT LOUD

I wander thro' each charter'd street,
Near where the charter'd Thames does flow.
And mark in every face I meet
Marks of weakness, marks of woe.
from "London" by William Blake

I had no idea where I was going
How I lived or what I did here
The yawning gulf between
Hangs like a rope from a wooden beam.
from "City of London" by the Mekons

Being neither a poet nor much of a lyricist, I feel like something of an interloper writing here in *Poetry*. For the last thirty years or so as a singer in the fundamentalist punk rock art project the Mekons, the occasional lyrics I have managed to cobble together make use of the long-standing Mekons' technique: blatant theft and collage. It's an old folk and blues method and if it's good enough for Bob Dylan then it's good enough for us. A Mekons songwriting session takes fragments from many sources: poetry, fiction (thank you, Herman Melville), nonfiction, lyrics from traditional songs where scraps and lines scrawled in Sharpie are bashed into shape by the band's magpies until something emerges that retains only a whiff of the original intent.

It's an effective way of working for a band that tries to write only when we are all in the same room and whose members are scattered across the United States, the UK, and Siberia. *Natural* (a record we released in 2007) was "a celebration of ritual, paganism and sacrifice" that we apparently wrote "after drinking whiskey all night, listening to the rocks and the Stones, tuning into strange, old frequencies, and reciting lines from Darwin and Thoreau," according to our press release at least. But you will find within it lines from or nods to Yeats's "broken boughs and blackened leaves," Baudelaire's "hunters lost in pathless woods," Emerson, the Talmud, and I Ching along with several others who may remain in copyright and therefore nameless.

Due to lack of time and money, Mekons recording sessions are quick affairs with little or no rehearsal. Often I sing the final version of a song a few minutes after the lyrics are finished and handed to me at the microphone. I then have to make sense of their meaning and how they fit the music. A singer has to use the sound of their voice and their phrasing to create an atmosphere, a little world, out of a few lines—and a singer for the Mekons has to do that with next to no preparation. My voice isn't particularly malleable or ornate, and I have a limited vocal range, but I'm lucky to have good tone and an ability to project emotion in a low-key way. It's doubtful I could work this way had I not spent so much time reading poetry aloud as a child.

> Look up and see the casement broken in,
> The bats and owlets builders in the roof!
> My cricket chirps against thy mandolin.
> Hush, call no echo up in further proof
> Of desolation! there's a voice within
> That weeps . . . as thou must sing . . . alone, aloof.
>
> from *Sonnets from the Portuguese* by Elizabeth Barrett Browning

Competitive poetry recitals were my first public performances, starting when I was about six years old and lasting until I lost interest, in my teens, after seeing David Bowie on *Top of the Pops*. Speech and drama festivals still take place all over the UK, though some seem to be part of a dying tradition. My local Wharfedale Festival is in its 109th year but now struggles to find entrants for its verse speaking classes. Perhaps the appeal has waned; children have other, more exciting things to do with their time and would rather not stand in drafty Victorian halls with their peers, reciting the same John Clare or Emily Dickinson poem to an audience of invested parents and a few pensioners looking for something to do on a rainy Saturday afternoon. My drama tutor, Angela Wayman, a strict woman who resembled a sexier version of Margaret Thatcher, would drill me after school in the stylings of Gerard Manley Hopkins or the structure of a sonnet. She would open the *Oxford Book of English Verse* and pick a random poem, and I'd attempt to deliver it without stumbling over the words or messing up the meter, and with as much feeling as I could muster on a first reading.

Nowadays I couldn't tell my iambic pentameter from my sprung rhythm, but when I open a book of poetry, if I am alone when I do, I always read the poem aloud to an imagined listener. Isn't that the intention, that the words are written to be heard? The techniques I learned "speaking" verse back then are the bedrock of my singing now: how to convey the mood of the song, where to place the emphasis, where to leave space, where the rhythm falls or where to battle it slightly for effect, how to use my voice in a way that brings the lyrics to life and adds a new element—all these things feel like second nature. The leap from reciting Hopkins to singing a Mekons song seems a short and easy one.

> Nothing is so beautiful as Spring—
> When weeds, in wheels, shoot long and lovely and lush.
>
> from "Spring" by Gerard Manley Hopkins

> A sparrow falls through dawn-air-mist
> Set in stone, searching for a signal.
>
> from "White Stone Door" by the Mekons

Whether it's finding the right tone for the spidery Mekons lyric that has just been thrust in front of me, reciting Dylan Thomas, Ivor Cutler, or some filthy limerick in the van on the way to a gig, or watching Jon Langford (fellow Mekon) stand behind a full-size cardboard cutout Dalek while reading John Donne's "The Good-Morrow" in a shrill, metallic voice as part of our Metaphysical Dalek Love Poetry series, poetry and Mrs. Wayman's stern eye continue to exert their subtle influence.

ANDERS NILSEN is an artist and author of several books, including *Poetry Is Useless*, *Rage of Poseidon*, and *The End*.

POETRY IS USELESS

POETRY.
WHAT THE HELL IS POETRY, ANYWAY?
POETRY POETRY POETRY
IT'S JUST ANOTHER WAY THE RULING CLASS MAINTAINS ITS
ANIMAL OPPENHEIMER COW'S MILK.
AND THE ONLY SURE WAY TO COLLAPSIBLE HAMBURGER CAMERA PHONE...
IS TO NOT ICEBURG LETTUCE TITANIUM LIVERSAUSAGE.
BECAUSE EVEN IF YOU RHINOPLASTY CHEW TOY...
...YOU'LL JUST PLAY INTO THEIR WHOLE HOSIERY COOKERY HELICOPTER
CELLAR DOOR?
APPLESAUCE CEILING FAN GARBAGE DUMP

05.09.08
IT HAS COME TO THE ATTENTION OF THE COMPTROLLER GENERAL THAT THERE IS SOME DISSENT AMONG THE RANKS ON THE SUBJECT OF POETRY AND ITS
USEFULNESS.
WHILE TRUE THAT SOME HEALTHY DIS-AGREEMENT ON A VARIETY OF ISSUES MAY BE IMPORTANT IN MAINTAINING A ROBUST DEMOCRATIC ATMOSPHERE...
THAT IS NOT TO SAY THAT THE READER SHOULD ENTERTAIN ANY ILLUSIONS THAT SUGGESTIONS OF POETRY'S UTILITY WILL BE GREETED BY THIS STRIP'S GOVERNING BODY AS ANY-THING OTHER THAN FANCIFUL DALLIANCE.
HEALTHY DEBATE IS ONE THING.
RIDICULOUS NONSENSE IS QUITE ANOTHER.
AND POT-ENTIALLY DANGEROUS RIDICULOUS NONSENSE WILL NOT BE TOLERATED.
THAT BEING SAID, WE WOULD, NONETHELESS, LIKE TO MAKE ONE CONCESSION TO THE DISSENTING PARTISAN'S POSITION.
POETRY MAY BE CONSIDERED TO HAVE ONE POTENTIAL USE.
TO BE BURNED FOR WARMTH.
THANK YOU. PLEASE PROCEED.

A good solid poem in your cortex can be almost like ballast in a ship's hold. If turbulent mental activity surges, speaking a poem to oneself can be a way to even out the waves.

JOSH WARN

Cartoonist and writer LYNDA BARRY has authored twenty-one books and received numerous awards and honors for her work. She is currently associate professor of interdisciplinary creativity and director of the Image Lab at the University of Wisconsin-Madison.

POETRY IS A DUMB-ASS SPIDER

Chicago hotel room, September 2009, fourteenth floor. Hungover and awake too early because of strong sun, at the window pulling down the shade, I see a spiderweb bigger than a dinner plate on the other side of the glass.

I think, Why there? You dumb-ass spider. What are your chances? How many bugs are flying around downtown at 140 feet? Why build your web almost flat against the glass when it reduces your capture area by half?

Back in bed, I think of being a bug in a windstorm blown straight toward the hotel window, knowing I'm going to die, preparing myself for impact, when I'm suddenly caught by a net at the last moment: the feeling of the miracle of this, of being saved, which turns quickly to the opposite of a miracle, which is being eaten alive.

Which death is worse?

And then the utilitarian thought: at least the bug did not go to waste.

And then the memory of the fellows who have been skinning human bodies and plasticizing their insides and putting them on display in action poses. There are shows of them that travel to museums and other venues, including one in Las Vegas. People can see the miracle of the actual human body: the arteries, veins, muscles, and tendons. It's not a somber display. Some of the bodies are running. Some are ice-skating. Some are throwing basketballs. Who are these people? And how did the skinner-men get so many of them?

And the memory of the photograph of the mobile execution trucks used in China, looking like recreational vehicles, rolling in a utilitarian way, cutting out the middleman, combining death sentence with pickup-and-delivery service and on-the-road organ harvesting.

And the memory of another photo taken in China on a cloudy day: two dead young men with wrists zip-tied behind their backs, lying naked in a driveway where a man is casually hosing them off like floor mats from a car.

And the memory of reading that the skinner-men get their bodies from China.

And a memory of accusations that the "researchers" had used political prisoners as the body source, a controversy over skinning and displaying people who had been put to death for their ideas. Then the utilitarian thought: the people who say, At least these bodies didn't go to waste. At least some scientific lemonade has been made out of a sour situation.

I am suddenly so thirsty and my head is pounding. I know the $9 beer in the minibar fridge will help. As I'm pouring it down my throat, a fragment of an A. E. Housman poem memorized two years ago presents itself as vividly as if someone were shouting it at me:

> When I watch the living meet,
> And the moving pageant file
> Warm and breathing through the street
> Where I lodge a little while,
>
> If the heats of hate and lust
> In the house of flesh are strong,
> Let me mind the house of dust
> Where my sojourn shall be long.

Only now it means the exact opposite of what I thought it meant. It's not about forbearance and taking the long view in life at all. It's saying, Life! Life! Get it while it's hot! I lift the beer can to that. To the dead A. E. Housman's still-living ideas.

And as the alcohol soothes me back into sleep, I think: What are the chances of a spider building a web against my hotel room window on the fourteenth floor while I drunkenly slept? How lucky I am! Not a dumb-ass spider at all. A genius spider. A genius spider speaking to me as clearly as the fictional Charlotte spoke to the fictional Wilbur. My eyes get wet. I lift my beer can toward the window. I say, "Some spider!" I sleep again.

What I don't know yet is that the spider I'm toasting is long gone, and that the web I thought was new is old and empty except for the tiny gray bodies a lot like ours wrapped tightly in the web's edges where we shall vibrate together in the useful wind until that moment when the poetry finally lets us go.

KAY REDFIELD JAMISON is a professor of psychiatry at the Johns Hopkins School of Medicine. Her books include *Nothing Was the Same*, *Exuberance: The Passion for Life*, and *Night Falls Fast: Understanding Suicide*.

WILD UNREST

I have found a kind of solace in poetry that I cannot find elsewhere. Perhaps it is because poetry so astutely conjures moods; moods, in turn, have determined so much of my life. I have had manic-depressive illness since I was seventeen; others in my family, many of my friends and colleagues, and most of my patients have suffered from mood disorders as well. Not surprisingly, much of my scientific and clinical writing has focused on trying to understand the psychology of normal and pathological moods—especially mania, depression, and "mixed states" (psychiatric conditions characterized by the simultaneous presence of both manic and depressive symptoms)—as well as attempting to elucidate the role of temperament and intense moods in artistic and scientific creativity.

At a personal level, I have turned time and again to poetry for comfort and understanding. As a clinician and teacher, I have used poetry to provide young doctors and graduate students with a deeper sense of the subjective experience of extreme mood states such as depression and mania. Both psychotherapists and psychopharmacologists need a more profound understanding of mood disorders than that which is presented, in staggeringly desiccated prose, in *The Diagnostic and Statistical Manual of Mental Disorders*, also known as the *DSM*, which is the foundation of clinical diagnosis in psychiatry and psychology.

It is essential that diagnosis be based on objective and rigorously researched criteria, of course. No patient is well served by subjectivity alone; empathy, while critical, will not in itself heal. Incorrect medication given on the basis of incorrect diagnosis is at best ineffective, and at worst dangerous. But a deeper understanding of psychological suffering must come from the experiences of those who have been there. Clearly, the most important sources for such knowledge are the words and clinical presentation of the patients themselves. But because patients may be too ill, disjointed, mute, or inarticulate to put into words experiences that are, under the best of circumstances, exceptionally difficult to describe, poetry can be an additional and powerful way to teach doctors (and, ultimately, the patients themselves) about disorders of mood.

Madness, and the agitation associated with madness, is nearly impossible to describe to those who have not experienced it. But poets do it remarkably well. I know of no better description of mania, for example, than Robert Lowell's pithy phrase that, when manic, one is "tireless, madly sanguine, menaced, and menacing." Likewise, Byron's description of madness as "a whirling gulf of phantasy and flame" rings painfully true for anyone who has lost access to reason. The violent perturbance usually present in mixed states and mania is brilliantly conveyed by poets who have known it firsthand. Thus Poe wrote of a "fearful agitation" that, left unchecked, would drive him "hopelessly mad," and Plath described in herself a violence as "hot as death-blood." Byron, who knew psychological and physical restlessness well, spoke of "the mind's canker in its savage mood," and Tennyson, in the wake of great grief, wrote brilliantly of "the wild unrest that lives in woe."

Depression, which is bloodlessly, if accurately, described by the *DSM* as "depressed mood or the loss of interest or pleasure in nearly all activities," is more humanly conveyed by William Cowper, in lines he wrote after a suicide attempt:

> encompass'd with a thousand dangers,
> Weary, faint, trembling with a thousand terrors,
> . . . .
> I, fed with judgment, in a fleshy tomb am
> Buried above ground.

Cowper catches the horror of depression, not just its symptoms. So too does Tennyson when he writes: "When the blood creeps, and the nerves prick / And tingle; and the heart is sick, / And all the wheels of Being slow." His portrayal of the melancholy of mourning is as clinically accurate as it is unforgettable.

Exaltation and expansiveness are hallmarks of the early stages of mania, but, as with depression, clinical texts find these psychological states difficult to convey. The great ecstatic poems of Delmore Schwartz and George Herbert, however, and those of Gerard Manley Hopkins, Dylan Thomas, and Walt Whitman, pulse with grandiosity and vitality. It may not be actual mania when Whitman writes,

> O the joy of my spirit—it is uncaged—it darts like lightning!
> It is not enough to have this globe or a certain time,
> I will have thousands of globes and all time.

But his poetry breathes what mania is all about.

Poets who themselves have been touched by despair or madness bring wisdom from the edge, not only to healers who would otherwise be untouched and uninformed, but to their patients who would otherwise be bereft of solace. I, like so many others who have been sick in mind, owe an inexpressible debt to poetry.

RICHARD RORTY (1931–2007) was an American philosopher. He served as professor emeritus of comparative literature at Stanford and was author of several books, including *Philosophy and the Mirror of Nature*.

THE FIRE OF LIFE

In an essay called "Pragmatism and Romanticism" I tried to restate the argument of Shelley's "Defense of Poetry." At the heart of Romanticism, I said, was the claim that reason can only follow paths that the imagination has first broken. No words, no reasoning. No imagination, no new words. No such words, no moral or intellectual progress.

I ended that essay by contrasting the poet's ability to give us a richer language with the philosopher's attempt to acquire nonlinguistic access to the really real. Plato's dream of such access was itself a great poetic achievement. But by Shelley's time, I argued, it had been dreamt out. We are now more able than Plato was to acknowledge our finitude—to admit that we shall never be in touch with something greater than ourselves. We hope instead that human life here on earth will become richer as the centuries go by because the language used by our remote descendants will have more resources than ours did. Our vocabulary will stand to theirs as that of our primitive ancestors stands to ours.

In that essay, as in previous writings, I used *poetry* in an extended sense. I stretched Harold Bloom's term "strong poet" to cover prose writers who had invented new language games for us to play—people like Plato, Newton, Marx, Darwin, and Freud as well as versifiers like Milton and Blake. These games might involve mathematical equations, or inductive arguments, or dramatic narratives, or (in the case of the versifiers) prosodic innovation. But the distinction between prose and verse was irrelevant to my philosophical purposes.

Shortly after finishing "Pragmatism and Romanticism," I was diagnosed with inoperable pancreatic cancer. Some months after I learned the bad news, I was sitting around having coffee with my elder son and a visiting cousin. My cousin (who is a Baptist minister) asked me whether I had found my thoughts turning toward religious topics, and I said no. "Well, what about philosophy?" my son asked. "No," I replied, neither the philosophy I had written nor that which I had read seemed to have any particular bearing on my situation. I had no quarrel with Epicurus's argument that it is irrational to fear death, nor with Heidegger's suggestion that ontotheology originates in an attempt to evade our mortality. But neither *ataraxia* (freedom from disturbance) nor *Sein zum Tode* (being toward death) seemed in point.

"Hasn't *anything* you've read been of any use?" my son persisted. "Yes," I found myself blurting out, "poetry." "Which poems?" he asked. I quoted two old chestnuts that I had recently dredged up from memory and been oddly cheered by, the most quoted lines of Swinburne's "Garden of Proserpine":

> We thank with brief thanksgiving
> Whatever gods may be
> That no life lives for ever;
> That dead men rise up never;
> That even the weariest river
> Winds somewhere safe to sea,

and Landor's "On His Seventy-Fifth Birthday":

> Nature I loved, and next to Nature, Art;
> I warmed both hands before the fire of life,
> It sinks, and I am ready to depart.

I found comfort in those slow meanders and those stuttering embers. I suspect that no comparable effect could have been produced by prose. Not just imagery, but also rhyme and rhythm were needed to do the job. In lines such as these, all three conspire to produce a degree of compression, and thus of impact, that only verse can achieve. Compared to the shaped charges contrived by versifiers, even the best prose is scattershot.

Though various bits of verse have meant a great deal to me at particular moments in my life, I have never been able to write any myself (except for scribbling sonnets during dull faculty meetings—a form of doodling). Nor do I keep up with the work of contemporary poets. When I do read verse, it is mostly favorites from adolescence. I suspect that my ambivalent relation to poetry, in this narrower sense, is a result of Oedipal complications produced by having had a poet for a father. (See James Rorty, *Children of the Sun* [Macmillan, 1926].)

However that may be, I now wish that I had spent somewhat more of my life with verse. This is not because I fear having missed out on truths that are incapable of statement in prose. There are no such truths; there is nothing about death that Swinburne and Landor knew but Epicurus and Heidegger failed to grasp. Rather, it is because I would have lived more fully if I had been able to rattle off more old chestnuts—just as I would have if I had made more close friends. Cultures with richer vocabularies are more fully human—farther removed from the beasts—than those with poorer ones; individual men and women are more fully human when their memories are amply stocked with verses.

MATT FITZGERALD is the senior pastor of Saint Paul's United Church of Christ in Chicago. He hosts the *Christian Century* magazine's *Preachers on Preaching* podcast and is a contributor to the *Stillspeaking Daily Devotional*.

GLORIOUSLY UNDONE

I am a preacher who has benefited greatly from reading poems. Poetry's forcefully expressive language and capacity for concise intelligence could benefit any minister, pressed as we are for time and inevitably lacking wisdom adequate to the odd and intense task before us. But there is another, far better reason for Christians to read poetry. Poems are often impenetrable, even baffling. The best poems seem to half grasp their own point, stretching past the limit of words into the place where language fails. Consider, for instance, this poem by the Tang Dynasty poet Wang Wei:

> On the branch tips the hibiscus bloom.
> The mountains show off red calices.
> Nobody. A silent cottage in the valley.
> One by one flowers open, then fall.
>
> "Magnolia Basin," translated by Barnstone et al.

What does the poem mean? Perhaps it says that death's hold over life limits our perspective, rendering us unable to experience even a decent trace of the wonder all around us. But the poem seems to stretch toward something more than this. It refuses my analysis, just sits there and shimmers and points past itself. I find it remarkable that language at its most sublime exposes its inadequacy most plainly.

And here, I think, is where poetry and Christianity share a powerfully true dynamic: both recognize a basic elusiveness; both testify to the fact that we see and don't see, seize and don't seize; both acknowledge a greater reality pulsing just beyond the boundary of the page, the poem, or even life itself.

Christianity rests on the belief that Jesus reveals God. And in contemporary America, Christianity's right wing has defined my religion as an arrogant sort of certainty. So it might sound odd to describe Christianity by its inability to reveal the whole of God. Yet this is the truth of Jesus Christ. In the thirties, in the face of Nazism's insistence that God was revealing His will through German history, Emil Brunner wrote: "Even Jesus Christ is . . . as Kierkegaard puts it, 'an indirect communication.' For direct communication is paganism. Direct communication cannot communicate the message of God, but only that of an idol."

We are too limited to understand the limitless. The only gods humanity can know inside and out are the ugly little pretenders that we shape to our own image, then send on our rotten errands. It is no accident that Christians convinced of their direct line of communication with God are always the first to draw the sword and bless our wars.

The Gospel of Mark says Jesus did not speak to his followers "except in parables." The one who came to reveal the truth of God did not speak except in riddles that bewilder even as they clarify. Jesus comes to show us who God is, yet in the very act of revelation he hides himself. As Karl Barth said, "God veils Himself precisely when he unveils, announces, and reveals Himself."

Veiling in the act of unveiling; truth revealed in a way that bewilders, even as it clarifies: to my ears, this sounds like a good definition of poetry. Or at least a definition of *good* poetry. For who wants to read a poem that is too easily understood? Such poems are like easily grasped gods, capable of carrying a message, perhaps, but not capable of pointing toward the truth. It seems to me that the beauty of the form is all tied up with a poem's refusal to be completely known.

We ache to know God completely, yet we cannot achieve such knowledge, and God does not give it to us. This is frustrating, but the alternative would be worse. Imagine how dull religion would be if we were able to understand every intricacy of God. Imagine how dull poetry would be if we were able to understand each poem in some exhaustive, ultimate way.

But there are dangers much worse than dullness. To know something completely is to control it, to command it, to subject it to our own ends. Just think of the horrors humanity would unleash were we able to master Divinity. Consider all the blood being shed by those who think they have—by a president who thinks he knows the mind of God and by terrorists who believe they are agents of heaven. They are all wrong, of course. But even something so flimsy as blood lust, projected onto heaven and confused with God's will, is strong enough to tear the world apart.

Poetry represents language at its zenith. And at their zenith, trying mightily to describe ultimate truth and beauty, our words grow thin and come gloriously undone. For ultimate truth is beyond our fallen capacity. And so, in an age of increasing religious certainty, poetry could be the very best thing for religious people to read. For even as they stun us with their power, great poems remind us of our inability to ever truly understand.

Civil rights attorney JERRY BOYLE works with Alvin Block & Associates in Chicago. He hails from a large family of Irish lawyers.

DEBRIS

Law is considered a scholarly profession, so we lawyers consider ourselves scholars. Worse, those of us who concentrate on litigating trials and appeals consider ourselves polymaths. A litigator's expertise is process, not substance, so we take any case that walks in the door, assuming we can master the substantive law with our scholarly erudition. It's no wonder we're notorious know-it-alls. And on no subject is our conceit more apparent than literature. We trade in words, so some of us fancy ourselves writers and, yes, even poets.

I have a friend I met as an adversary—we tried a case together, on opposite sides. Flaubert presumably intended the pejorative connotation of "every lawyer bears within him the debris of a poet" for lawyers like my friend—he always wants to talk about literature, and I oblige him. But while my former adversary has forgiven me for besting him in the courtroom, he will never forgive me for admitting that, no, I don't love literature for its own sake, but rather because it sharpens my persuasive rhetoric. He contends I'm abusing my "creative talents" by practicing law, but I'm quite certain he's projecting. I am a lawyer first, foremost, and always. For me, literature serves the law, not the other way around. As I see it, Flaubert couldn't cut it in law school anyway and dropped out, leaving lawyers to resolve the denotation of his poetic debris. We take out the poet's trash.

Poets have the luxury of posing questions because the consequences of poetic equivocation are abstract. But lawyers are compelled to pose answers, because lawsuits result in unequivocal judgments which deprive our clients of life, liberty, or property. T. S. Eliot, a banker, was presumably familiar with the Golden Rule: if you have the gold, you make the rules. Bankers draft their documents with a relentless precision designed to reserve every advantage to the lender. But the lender's advantage is often purloined by the borrower's lawyer in litigation. In one case, I focused on an errant comma, resulting in a dangling modifying clause, upon which the whole case hung. Judges and juries don't give "maybe" for an answer, so I argued the doctrine of the last antecedent, and that dangling clause fell to earth with a crushing blow on the bank's position.

I suspect it was experiences like that that induced banker Eliot to bemoan "the intolerable wrestle / With words and meanings." I know it was poet Eliot who taught me that you can never really be sure what the meaning of *is* is:

> Words strain,
> Crack and sometimes break, under the burden,
> Under the tension, slip, slide, perish,
> Decay with imprecision, will not stay in place,
> Will not stay still.
>
> from "Burnt Norton"

Lawyers have a lot to learn from poets. I credit the Oulipian Raymond Queneau for my appreciation and, more important, comprehension of what is perhaps the longest sentence in the legal canon, section 341(e) of the Internal Revenue Code. Try making sense of a sentence with 435 words preceding the main verb without a perverse appreciation for arbitrary constraints. That's a dare, in case you were wondering.

Or try convincing a tribunal that it's all right for a raunchy magazine to publish long-forgotten salacious photos of a now-famous actress without her permission. Well, the photos previously appeared in another (albeit less vulgar) magazine, so republication hardly invaded her privacy. And the text appended to the photos, while suggestive, was hardly libelous. Wallace Stevens cut right to the heart of the case:

> I do not know which to prefer,
> The beauty of inflections
> Or the beauty of innuendoes,

The blackbird whistling
Or just after.

from "Thirteen Ways of Looking at a Blackbird"

Unlike Flaubert, Stevens graduated from law school and practiced law. He fairly presented both sides of the dispute but surely knew, deep in his dark lawyer's heart, that the only choice is, precisely, both. So do I. Sometimes the clients are just wrong, and there's not much we can do. We're not poets, so we know we can't win every time. All we can do is dispose of the poets' debris.

JOSH WARN is a retired member of Ironworkers Local Union 25, Detroit. He lives in Ypsilanti, Michigan, where he writes about Michigan history and the fascinating year 1919.

ON THE ROAD WITH WALLACE AND WYSTAN

I accepted a correction from Wallace Stevens with only a bit of quibbling. Apparently he hadn't realized how evocative and olfactory the word "brewing" could be in "The Idea of Order at Key West," where he had used "heaving" instead. In committing the poem to memory I had repeated scores of times:

> It would have been deep air,
> The brewing speech of air, a summer sound
> Repeated in a summer without end.

When I finally looked at a text and saw "heaving" it was a bit wrenching, but I let Wallace have his way.

My emendation—or, if you insist, my mistake—came from having memorized "The Idea of Order" by glancing at its lines handwritten on the backs of business cards while cruising east on the Ohio Turnpike. Memorizing and reciting was a way I passed some hours of the biweekly commute in the company F-350, slouching toward Buffalo loaded with the steel construction paraphernalia that my ironworker colleagues call "ten pounds of shit in a five pound box."

The truck and its boxes might look like a mess to strangers, but I've worked to keep some sense to it. The order of a tightly crafted poem has the same kind of appeal to me. The job site might be dirty, noisy, and cold, losing money and behind schedule, but I feel better knowing which box holds the three-quarter-inch drive sockets. Maybe Stevens speaks to a similar need when he writes about the senses overwhelmed by

> Theatrical distances, bronze shadows heaped
> On high horizons, mountainous atmospheres
> Of sky and sea

and about humans wanting to find or manufacture order in untamable nature, like his narrator, who recalls the lights on tilting fishing boats as the stylus of a giant compass, maybe even a wand, "Fixing emblazoned zones and fiery poles, / Arranging, deepening, enchanting night." Well, my truck was not as wild as Stevens's Caribbean scenes, nor is my crafty arrangement of gear equivalent to the transformative art of the poem's heroine:

> when she sang, the sea,
> Whatever self it had, became the self
> That was her song, for she was the maker.

Ironwork is often artful though, if not arty, and there are reasons that carrying longish poems in memory has some of the same satisfactions as completing a difficult weld or fitting a steel handrail to a curved stair. For one thing, when you haul out a poem from the brain's back room, it feels like you own it. Each time you run through it you see different inflections you might use. Though the copyright owner might disagree, you share in his or her creative expression. On a long walk, for instance, you might try out seven different ways to enunciate Stevens's image of the willful, senseless sea: "Like a body wholly body, fluttering / Its empty sleeves."

This possessing of poems may have benefits, but probably not social ones. You might impress people at certain parties, but they're likely just literary types, and trying to impress that bunch is what got me into this manual-labor mess. Or so I've heard myself say as I've pondered, while clinging to some icy, skinny beam with my fingers, how differently life might have turned out if I'd studied harder for my chemistry final instead of pulling an all-nighter on that Yeats paper. On the other hand, I dared once to start reciting W. H. Auden's "The Shield of Achilles" on a construction site, because the young guy dragging welding cables with me was mouthing one of Eminem's clever raps. After a couple of lines, I saw Auden wasn't matching my partner's Red Bull rhythms, so I switched over to "Subterranean Homesick Blues." The kid wasn't listening to that ancient stuff either, but it didn't matter, because the floor grinders started their machine and nobody could hear anything.

So I still haven't impressed anyone beyond family, but reciting from memory has other benefits. A good solid poem in your cortex can be almost like ballast in a ship's hold. If turbulent mental activity surges, speaking a poem to oneself can be a way to even out the waves. I first learned this through my practice of memorizing Psalms. But even nominally secular poems recited aloud soothe, and not merely by providing a distraction from disturbing matters, but by the steady rhythm of their sound, and their effects on the breath. Consider even these dark words from "The Shield of Achilles":

> An unintelligible multitude,
> A million eyes, a million boots in line,
> Without expression, waiting for a sign.
> . . . .
> Column by column in a cloud of dust
> They marched away enduring a belief
> Whose logic brought them, somewhere else, to grief.

In speaking the poem's sixty-seven lines you restrain yourself from the familiar flurries of contemporary mediaspeak and follow phrasings that come from a deeper place.

But pleasure may be the main reason I keep memorizing poems. The intense familiarity of a work known by heart allows happy moments of sensing the poem as a whole and in details. This pleasure is not simply the kick of solving a puzzle, nor my ironworker affinity for structure. There is also pleasure in sounds and rhythms, even the mouth pleasure of "unintelligible multitude." But at its best the experience of a good poem has to do with trying to apprehend a deeply known truth that another person could communicate only with a precise set of words. Probably I like both "The Shield of Achilles" and "The Idea of Order at Key West" because in each such a valuable perception underlies the art, making them not only good company on a long drive, but worth the effort to learn.

XENI JARDIN is founding partner and coeditor of the blog *Boing Boing*, and executive producer and host of Webby-honored *Boing Boing Video*. She is a frequently sought tech expert in TV news.

EVERYTHING MOVES TO LIVE

Sometimes reality is too complex for oral communication. But legend embodies it in a form which enables it to spread all over the world.

ALPHA 60, the IBM mainframe villain, *Alphaville*

Alphaville is my favorite film. It has become more of a personal totem than a favorite film, really. It's a code I carry around with me, like the encryption strings my hacker friends store on USB key fobs and wear around their necks. I first saw it in the early nineties, around the same time I started working with computers. I grew up in a family of painters, poets, and musicians, so aligning with machines felt like a thrilling "fuck you" to my family at the time.

But *Alphaville* merged those seemingly opposing realms in a way that mirrors my life now, and the way I have come to understand what life is: there is poetry in the network. There is math in music. Metal dreams of becoming a spaceship. And the spaceship dreams of flying toward stars.

The film follows the tale of Lemmy Caution (Eddie Constantine), a hard-boiled, trench coat–wearing film noir detective sent to the city of Alphaville to rescue its citizens (many of whom, conveniently, happen to be total babes) from the techno-totalitarian clutches of an evil IBM mainframe computer. Love is illegal in the dictatorship of Alpha 60. Expressing grief, desire, or tenderness, even reading poetry, these are all crimes punishable by death—specifically, staged executions in which prisoners are lined up and shot on the edge of a swimming pool filled with synchronized Busby Berkeley–style bathing beauties.

"What transforms darkness into light?" Alpha 60 asks Lemmy Caution during a grim interrogation scene.

"La poésie," he answers.

In *Alphaville*, poetry is emotional code that unlocks freedom. Throughout, Jean-Luc Godard references the work of Argentinean poet Jorge Luis Borges and his contemporary, the French surrealist Paul Éluard. The film's opening line, referenced above, was inspired by Borges's essay "Forms of a Legend."

Éluard's 1926 collection *Capital of Pain* is the book that an underground poet-friend passes in secret to Caution, a book that Caution in turn passes on to Natacha von Braun (Anna Karina), the beautiful daughter of the evil scientist who designed and programmed Alpha 60.

In what I have always believed is the film's most transcendent and beautiful scene, Natacha clutches Éluard's book to her chest. She is delivering a dream-soliloquy that I understand is a translation from Éluard's 1924 work *Mourir de ne pas mourir* (Dying of not dying):

> Because I love you, everything moves
> We must advance to live
> Aim straight ahead toward those you love
>
> I went toward you, endlessly toward the light
> If you smile, it enfolds me all the better
> The rays of your arms pierce the mist.

I have played this film and read selections from those Éluard collections for each person I've fallen in love with over the last twenty years (not that there have been so many of them). They express for me, better than my own words can, what it means to submit to the vulnerability that love requires. They capture what it means to accept that control and order are illusion, never mind what technology promises; chaos and chance are the magic in intimacy. They remind me of the eventuality of pain that any deep bond with another person entails, no matter how rich and blissful the sweet parts are.

The last guy who sat through *Alphaville* with me, who tolerated my reading Éluard stanzas over Skype in bad French, who received my copy-pasted Borges passages over IM late at night—he was the first who really understood them. And, I think, the first who really understood me. I didn't intend the Godard-Éluard Test as a test, but I suppose it ended up being one. Because he really is a keeper.

I am not a poet. I am a blogger. We bloggers suffer less and earn more than poets. We are more vain and less patient. The work we produce may yield quick rewards and praise, but our output fades just as quickly into the infinitely expanding black hole of Google. What poets produce is less easily found, but endures the fickle flow of mediums, each eclipsing the last.

My creative mentor, the poet who adopted me as a teen and taught me all I know about writing, tells me this: "Poetry is not adornment. Poetry is the truth." Poetry is, you might say, the command-line prompt of the human operating system, a stream of characters that calls forth action, that elicits response. Lemmy Caution knew this when he recited Borges to hack Alpha 60 and win the heart of his chosen babe.

For poetry is against gravity. Reading Walt Whitman, Pablo Neruda, Federico García Lorca, and Vladimir Mayakovsky at a young age, I discovered that all poetry has the same quality. It transports us to another place, away from the moment, away from our circumstances.

AI WEIWEI

AMY FRYKHOLM is the author of three books of nonfiction, including *See Me Naked: Stories of Sexual Exile in American Christianity*. She currently edits the media column at the *Christian Century*.

EARTHWARD

Rusanna and I sit at my linoleum-topped kitchen table with the oven door propped open for heat. On the table in front of us are half-drunk cups of sugared tea and copies of Marina Tsvetaeva's poem "Uzh Skol'ko Ikh" (Already how many). Rusanna is coaching me to read it in Russian. She is a painstaking teacher of pronunciation, correcting all of my soft and hard *ts*, my improperly rounded vowels, my strewn accents. But she is also moody and distractible. She interrupts our lesson to say, "Tell me about how American men make love." When I confess that, at twenty-one, I have never had any lovers, American or otherwise, she scoffs and then pouts: "Why don't you tell me the truth? I tell you everything. Everyone knows that American girls have more lovers than anyone."

Disappointed in love, Rusanna imagines that the country of Montana and John Wayne has men to equal her passion. She takes my reticence on the subject as selfish—I want all the men for myself, she says. We reach this impasse again and again. In our youth and vanity, we are like the poem's speaker:

All will grow cold
that once sang and struggled
glistened and rejoiced
the green of my eyes,
the gold of my hair
my gentle voice

Rusanna is Armenian. My kitchen table is in Estonia, where Rusanna is raising her daughter and I am teaching English. We are studying Russian almost covertly because both of us know that Estonian would be more useful and certainly more politically correct. But both of us have also become obsessed with the idea that I might pronounce *myagkiznak* with just the right softness. Truth be told, Rusanna hates the Estonian language, Estonian winters, and, not least of all, Estonian men, whom she finds cold and unfeeling. I have become her repository for these complaints on the long, dark nights of winter, and in the meantime I recite and memorize "Uzh Skol'ko Ikh" until its forms are so familiar I feel they have entered my cells. The door to the Russian language creaks open under Rusanna's instruction, and I whisper the words of the poem on the bus, at the market, and as I fall asleep.

I did not grasp at first that Russian would be best learned through its poetry. I memorized grammar structures and vocabulary lists. I treated the language like a fill-in-the-blank exercise, but when I arrived in Russia for the first time in my junior year of college, communication eluded me. After two years of study, no one understood me when I ordered bread at a bakery or wished a friend happy birthday. Near despair, I sat one day in phonetics class while the teacher tried to prod her American students to hear the melodies of the Russian language. We rehearsed the same sentence over and over again, testing different intonation patterns. Suddenly I understood. Russian was first and foremost a music. To speak it, you had to learn to sing it.

The Russian language and Russian poetry are inextricably linked. Russians memorize dozens of poems. They employ poems in arguments and recite them on street corners. Their poets are beloved authorities on any subject. In 1991, when I went to study in a provincial Russian city, I was invited to an elementary school so that the children could meet an actual American. "Be alert, children," the teacher said. "This will be the only opportunity you may ever have to see an American." Then she demanded that I recite a poem in English so they could hear my "American speech." I did not know how to explain that Americans don't typically recite poems—maybe nursery rhymes, maybe a line or two memorized in high school. But beyond "Hickory Dickory Dock," we are an impoverished people.

To my relief, I had recently, in a lovesick state, memorized Robert Frost's "To Earthward," and I was able to recite at least part of it while the children stared at me uncomprehendingly. They sensed the lack of authority I brought to the recitation. It was that, as much as the foreign language, that befuddled them.

I have never stopped turning to Russian poems. Tsvetaeva was the first. But like a dog with a bone, I bury Russian poems in my subconscious and bring them out to chew on. I've buried Anna Akhmatova's simple, earthy phrases like those she wrote upon learning of the arrest of her son:

U menya sevodnya mnogo delo:
Nado pamyat' do kontsa ubit',
Nado, chtob dusha okamenela
Nado snova nauchit'sya zhit'

Today I have a lot to do
I must destroy all my memory
I must turn my soul to stone
I must learn again how to live
from "The Sentence"

Or Mandelstam's aching fluidity, or the poem-songs of Yuri Shevchuk from the rock group DDT. Whenever I am lonely or tired, have a painful commute, cannot sleep, or lose the thread of my life, these poems, written in a language that even after two decades of study I only slightly comprehend, serve as touchstones. My very inability to master their meanings or even to perfect my *t*s serves a mysterious, orienting purpose beyond the knowledge of my mouth or consciousness. These poems stir what the visionary Julian of Norwich called my "love-longing." They remain always just beyond my reach.

DANIEL HANDLER is the author of the novels *The Basic Eight*, *Watch Your Mouth*, *Adverbs*, and far too many books as Lemony Snicket, including *13 Words*, with Maira Kalman.

HAPPY, SNAPPY, SAPPY

If you were to walk into my living room on some weekend night, that would be creepy. But before I stood up alarmed and demanded to know what you were doing there, you would see me in a big black leather chair that, I've been told, is too big for the room. I'd be all dressed up, and reading poetry.

I've never had any of the problems with poetry that most people do, i.e., that it's boring and/or incomprehensible. A voracious reader, I spent my childhood reading things for adults, and learned early to find peace in the stasis of literature. Having read *The Rainbow* at fourteen (I'd heard D. H. Lawrence was dirty), a Robert Hass poem feels action packed. And as far as comprehension goes, I find poetry actually has very little mystery compared to anything else. Just this morning at the bus stop, a little electronic sign told me my bus was arriving in two minutes, then one minute, then "arriving," although the street remained empty. Then it was gone. I'd missed a bus that had never arrived. Not a phrase in Ashbery's "The Tennis Court Oath" can touch that for sheer befuddlement.

My problem with poetry was *when* to read it—for pleasure, I mean. I know how to read poetry when studying it (Donne out loud in my dorm room, for instance, with my college girlfriend feigning interest); I know how to read it when trying to write it (I ripped off so much of the collected Bishop that she really should have been awarded the 1992 Connecticut Student Poet Prize instead of, ahem, me); and I know how to read it when I'm reviewing it (in three long sittings at my local bar, with bourbon deliciously swaying my critical opinions). When I'm Lemony Snicket, I most surely know how to read *Les fleurs du mal* to tatters while writing thirteen books about terrible things happening to orphans I named Baudelaire in what the French call *hommage*. But until a few years ago, I was having trouble figuring out when to read poetry when I just wanted to *read*.

With the huge tomes, there was simply no way. I'd buy them when they came out—so handsome and hefty that there was a great promise that, as with handsome and hefty people, they'd fix everything right away. But at home they were daunting, unhelped by reviews implying that we've all memorized Czeslaw Milosz—ah, yes, "Unde Malum"—and that they should squat on the shelves just for "reference." But even with a standard volume—you know, about eight years of work for some poets, or a week and a half for Charles Simic—there are only so many poems by a single poet one can read in a sitting. I read two or three poems by Campbell McGrath in a row, and I'm infused with joy at the enthusiasm of his breadth. I read seven or eight, and it is truly admirable that he can maintain a consistency of tone and yet always be surprising. Ten or twelve and that just might be enough Campbell McGrath for a little bit, no offense. Eighteen poems without a break and seriously, Campbell, shut the fuck up. What to do?

The answer came, as so many answers do, from my wife one Saturday night. It's an unfair world, and like most of my gender I can go from listening to Sonic Youth in my sweatpants to showered, shaved, and dressed to the nines, ready for the first martini, in fifteen minutes—twenty with a Windsor knot. My wife, meanwhile, has the patriarchy to contend with and so, in order to emerge in formal loveliness despite my protests that she looks equally ravishing in a ravished cardigan, requires all the time that there is. This left me at odds one too many times. What to do while waiting for her? There's drink, but there's enough of that ahead. There's a child, but he's covered in miso soup and blaming the babysitter. There's e-mail, but how can I claim *I can't possibly*, *I don't have the time*, while replying on a Saturday night? "Get out of here," my wife said when I went to remind her that if we didn't leave we risked being only twenty minutes early. "Go sit in that chair you insisted on buying that is really too big for the room."

I did, and impulsively grabbed the complete poems of Cesare Pavese. In the bedroom my wife turned on the hair dryer for the third time. "Stunned by the world," I read,

I reached an age
when I threw punches at air and cried to myself.
Listening to the speech of women and men,
not knowing how to respond, it's not fun.
But this too has passed: I'm not alone anymore,
and if I still don't know how to respond,
I don't need to. Finding myself, I found company.

from "Ancestors"

I kept going and I keep going. I'd found a perfect slice of time, as suited for poetry as—you say it, Matthea Harvey—the bathtub is for the human form. I first read Harvey this way, and Chelsey Minnis, and Joshua Beckman. I've furrowed through Joshua Clover and raged and raved with Carolyn Kizer. I get snappy with D. A. Powell and happy with James Tate and sappy with Robert Frost. I admire the designs from Wave Books and Ugly Duckling Presse. I try not to let Daisy Fried make me too weepy or Anne Carson make me feel too dim, and I try, again and again, to make legitimate headway with *The Changing Light at Sandover* because it's been twenty years and I'm as lost as the earring my darling can't find. The world doesn't quite stop while I read, but my space in it is unaccounted for—what better context can one ask for to understand *For the Fighting Spirit of the Walnut*? I invite everyone who's dressed and ready to join me. Despite rumor, there's plenty of space in the living room, even with my chair. Which you should get out of. It's mine.

MICHAELANNE PETRELLA is coauthor of the children's book *Recipe* and writes Internet things you bookmarked but didn't read. She lives in the San Francisco Bay Area.

LIKE, A NOTICEABLE AMOUNT OF PEE

My experience of poetry has always been confined to school, with one exception. My dad made me memorize Robert Louis Stevenson's "Time to Rise" when I was ten. It was a very hilarious inside joke that he and my mom had about shaming me into waking up before noon. Beyond that, elementary school introduced me to a whole world of poems that rhymed with cat and bat. Most of the poems that I wrote at that time were either scary or funny, and nothing in between: poetry, for me, was either a series of ominous terror "images" or rhyming poems making fun of school lunch meat.

It wasn't until college that I really tangled with poetry. I hadn't been looking forward to my poetry classes at first, but by being forced to take them I found that certain kinds of poetry resonated. For instance, haiku class was one of my favorites because it allowed for strange wording. We could write whatever we wanted within the standard haiku form. We were encouraged to mimic the greats like Buson or Bashō, and invoke natural images and subtle wisdom. I remember liking haiku, but not necessarily for its wisdom. I liked the *sound* of translation. When it was translated, it sounded almost Jedi-like. There was this famous haiku by Issa:

> Don't kill that fly!
> Look—it's wringing its hands,
> wringing its feet.

I remember thinking that I wanted everything I wrote to sound like that; I wanted my poems to have a Björk-like lyric quality, where everything was so oddly specific, but at the same time, inappropriately funny.

Many of my haikus went like this:

Baby in the yard.
Where is the baby's holder?
Holding the cell phone.

Or:

Mashed cantaloupe soup
It does not taste like you'd think
Unfortunately

Or:

There is a stupid
Stupidly stupid stupid
Stupid stupid horse.

Often I would get a laugh from one or more students, and almost always a laugh from the professor (of course, not without obligatory head shaking that signified fake admonishment). I found that most people actually appreciated humor in poems. There was a willing audience, eager to hear something that didn't make them sad or bored. Most of the students' poems were about death, grandma, grandma's death, rain, or questions about life, all of which were overwrought, indulging in clichés and dramatic description. Many poems were thinly-veiled confessions or metaphors by way of rain or wound imagery. Sometimes it rained directly inside of the wounds. Sometimes the rain was hurtful. Sometimes the wound itself rained blood onto their cheekbones, which implied eye blood, I guess.

In our most emotional moments, we don't tend to edit. I found that funny poetry worked well because it was all about editing and timing. Much of my time was spent whittling down the exact joke, or emotion, that I was trying to convey. The best moment from class was when I read a particularly short poem that ended with the lines, "When my dog Pepper peed in the pool. Like, a noticeable amount of pee." It got a laugh, but the laughter felt like a big sigh of relief. It was the last poem read aloud during a day of dead grandma poems, but it was also a textbook example of solid editing.

My professor pointed to various parts of my poem where I could have elaborated and how that would have basically killed the punch line. She said that in its simplicity, the emotion was stronger and, as a result, the reaction greater. We had a group discussion about editing, timing, and the word *pee*.

Learning to make poetry funny gave me invaluable editing experience. I found an ally in poetry: I know my experience with it helps to inform my editing and makes me, I hope, a funnier writer. Polonius said it best, during his ironically rambling preface in *Hamlet*: "Brevity is the soul of wit." Or as my incisive professor would say, "Brevity = Wit." So keeping that wisdom in mind, I'll end this in the same way: Good poetry = Edited poetry.

AI WEIWEI is an artist who resides and works in Beijing. He is an outspoken advocate of human rights and freedom of speech.

ON POETRY

My father, Ai Qing, was an early influence of mine. He was a true poet, viewing all subjects through an innocent and honest lens. For this, he suffered greatly. Exiled to the remote desert region of Xinjiang, he was forbidden to write. During the Cultural Revolution, he was made to clean the public toilets. At the time, those rural toilets were beyond one's imagination, neglected by the entire village. This was as low as one's condition could go. And yet, as a child I saw him making the greatest effort to keep each toilet as clean and as pleasant as possible, taking care of the waste with complete sincerity. To me, this is the best poetic act, and one that I will never forget.

My father was punished for being a poet, and I grew up in its consequences. But even when things were at their most difficult, I saw his heart protected by an innocent understanding of the world. For poetry is against gravity. Reading Walt Whitman, Pablo Neruda, Federico García Lorca, and Vladimir Mayakovsky at a young age, I discovered that all poetry has the same quality. It transports us to another place, away from the moment, away from our circumstances.

In my own work, the process of creation always requires the understanding of aesthetics in relation to morality, to the pureness of a form, or to a personal language, one which extends us clearly to another. Many of my projects have poetic elements. In 2007, I brought 1,001 Chinese citizens to Kassel, Germany, for *documenta* 12. For many, it was their first time traveling outside of China. This was *Fairytale*. In 2008, we researched, under extremely harsh and restrictive conditions, the aftermath of the Great Sichuan Earthquake and unearthed the names and birth dates of 5,196 student victims, otherwise buried forever.

I used to say that Twitter is the perfect form for poetry. It is the poetry of society in the modern age. In engaging social media and the forms of communication it makes possible, again and again we find ourselves deeply moved with emotion. By anger, joy, even feelings that are new and indescribable. This is poetic. It makes today a unique time.

To experience poetry is to see over and above reality. It is to discover that which is beyond the physical, to experience another life and another level of feeling. It is to wonder about the world, to understand the nature of people, and, most importantly, to be shared with another, old or young, known or unknown.

CHRISTOPHER HITCHENS (1949–2011) was a journalist and columnist for magazines such as *New Statesman*, the *Nation*, *Slate*, and *Vanity Fair*. His many books include *Cyprus*, *God Is Not Great: How Religion Poisons Everything*, and *Arguably: Essays*.

IMPERFECT RECALL

My own acquaintance and relationship with poetry is bound up with acquisition, memorization, and recital. That is: I realized when I was quite young that I could learn poems "by heart," as the saying goes. This may have something to do with early experience in compulsory religious and scriptural studies. It was no hardship for me to commit hymns and verses of the Bible (though not so many psalms, oddly enough) to memory. Furthermore, I found that this fairly simple attainment could, as well as give me satisfaction, win me praise. This helped make up for my almost dyslexic inability to read music or play a note on any instrument. And when it came to poetry, I would squirm at the embarrassed clumsiness with which my classmates "read" beautiful lines that they obviously felt were effeminate by definition.

Not that there was anything effeminate about the sort of verse upon which I cut my teeth. Originating from a naval family, and brought up in all-boys boarding schools, I was full of Henry Newbolt and Rudyard Kipling and Thomas Babington Macaulay. Even cornier heroic and patriotic poems and songs have a hold on me to this day. (The hymns and Bible verses have lost their grip, without being forgotten.) This helped rather than hindered my later exposure to W. H. Auden and Wilfred Owen, the latter of whose poems had the effect of a swift uppercut to my chin. It wasn't easy to "learn" all ninety-nine lines of "September 1, 1939," though I can still get through it if I have a prompter, but Owen's "Dulce Et Decorum Est" is one of the poems I take with me everywhere and don't need to look up. By a useful coincidence, Cecil Day-Lewis was an "old boy" of the prep school at which my father worked after he left the Royal Navy, and the first time I ever had a book signed was by this quasi-mythical figure of "The Thirties." He had come, as he did every year, to judge the school's "poetry saying" competition. I thought then, and think now, that there was value in that name for it.

At any rate, I suppose that Homer would have approved. And probably Shakespeare, too. I cannot claim much authority for myself, but I think that there is something of the gold standard about the echo and recall of poetry in the conscious mind. For example, I could now argue from various positions that Ezra Pound was a lousy poet as well as a depraved pseudo-intellectual (especially after reading the muscular treatment accorded him, for his classical solecisms alone, by Robert Conquest). But I "knew" this as soon as I opened Pound's books and saw the sinister gibberish on the page. I am forced to concede that he must have "had" something as an editor, since I cannot imagine life without some of Eliot's choruses or Yeats's "An Irish Airman Foresees His Death," and since both men acknowledged his help and advice. Poetry, to put it another way, is also a good training in the ironic.

Book signings and encounters to one side (I heard Auden read "On the Circuit" in Great St. Mary's Church in Cambridge in its year of publication), the first true poet I ever met was James Fenton, who was my contemporary at Oxford. He had won early fame and a prize for a sonnet sequence, but he was forever composing bits of blues, along with parodies and what he sometimes called "rude songs." This proved to be equally true, as I got older and got to know them, of Robert Conquest and Kingsley Amis. A preferred form was the limerick, of which I still have a hundred or so hardwired into my cortex in case of need (or opportunity). Not all these need be filthy—I have a special reserve of clean ones, some without even a double entendre—but all of them do need to follow a certain simple but exacting scheme. It depresses me beyond measure that most people I meet cannot even recite, much less compose, this gem-like form. Nor can any student in any of my English classes produce a single sonnet of Shakespeare: not even to get themselves laid (the original purpose of the project).

I worry that by phrasing things in this way I may myself be adding to the general coarsening and deafness. Of course my test isn't the one true test: who can safely say that they have memorized *Don Juan*, for instance? But then who could you count as reliable who could not manage a stave or two of *The Waste Land*? The word *Koran* means "the recitation," and it seems that in Arabic its incantation can induce trance by sheer power and beauty. (Auden was wrong, in his valediction for Yeats, to say that "poetry makes nothing happen.") At least this restores the idea of a relationship to the theoretically divine, and to the audience. (Auden also wrote of Yeats that "mad Ireland hurt you into poetry," which at any rate implies the possibility of a reciprocal relationship between poetry and the reality of which Eliot believed that "human kind" could not bear too much.)

Yet very often, late at night, when I am not tired enough for sleep but too tired to carry on with absorbing or apprehending anything "serious" or new, I will walk over to the appropriate shelf and pull out the tried and the true: the ones that never fail me. And then I will always stay up even later than I had intended. And sometimes, in the morning, I really can "do" the whole of "Spain 1937" or "The Road to Mandalay," and can appreciate that writing is not just done by hand.

The purpose of "our" reality is to cover up the fact of death, and one of the things writers and poets can—and should—do is to unpack the lies of reality, beginning with the lie of life eternal in the present.

ALEKSANDAR HEMON

There is magic in hearing voices speaking out for justice over the din of a bustling city.

MARIAME KABA

ETIENNE NDAYISHIMIYE is a Twa parliamentarian in the East Central African nation of Burundi. Founder of UNIPROBA, a human rights nonprofit advocating for Batwa equality, he also serves on the board of Community for Burundi.

DUST AND STONES

There is a certain romance to poetry of witness, poetry of prisoners and the oppressed, scrawled with fingernails into Styrofoam cups in Guantanamo. But that romance, in my experience, is just that. Most of my people, the Batwa, don't engage in any way with the type of poetry published in this magazine—because when it comes down to poetry and food, survivors choose food.

Most Westerners are familiar with the Hutus and Tutsis as a result of the media blitz that followed the Rwandan genocide of the early nineties. Fewer are aware that a third tribe exists, mine. The Batwa are the original inhabitants of East Central Africa, first colonized by the agriculturalist Hutus at the turn of the first millennium, later by the cattle-herding Tutsis in the 1400s. Commonly called pygmies, a term we now reject as derogatory, we share ancestry with other indigenous populations of Africa, like the |xam of South Africa, who left behind a notable body of poetry, transcribed by their diligent friend Wilhelm Bleek, a Prussian linguist and pioneering ethnographer. Like the displaced |xam, we too are landless, forced to move at our government's whim from squat to squat of unfertile land.

The Batwa are not a people without poetry—that is far from true—but we have been forced by the socioeconomic realities we face to articulate our poetry differently. The primary barrier between literary poetry and us is the problem of our overwhelming illiteracy, at an international high of at least 90%. Still, we are a people of singing and dancing, and we sing at every opportunity: while hunting, fishing, while selling our pottery at the market, and even more so at occasions calling for great ceremony, like weddings and births—especially twins! Our poetry is in that way much more communal, much more essential than any written verse, and we could not survive without it.

One of my favorite poems from childhood exemplifies our oral poetry. Political in the sense that it accurately reflects our forced engagement with poverty and social injustice, the poem is well known in our communities:

> I want to sing to the memory of my beloved father
> who gave me a beautiful, special cow
> so I could walk slender-hipped like a handsome prince
> before my unjust murder.

There are a few of us Batwa who have finished secondary school, and seven of our one hundred thousand have attended college. I was born in 1964 in Ruziba, a rural province of Burundi thirteen kilometers from Bujumbura, along Lake Tanganyika. I began school at age seven, but in my second year of primary school, in 1971, an ethnic crisis brought on a full civil war. During this time I fled to the Democratic Republic of the Congo, where I lived alone as a refugee for three years. As a young child, I survived on the street, doing the small jobs I could find. During that time I clung to a particularly poetic song for refugees, often sung at churches in the original Kirundi:

> Tamba Imana Yawe
> Tamba Imana Yawe
> Aho wabunda mu bisaka
> Ninde yahagukuye,

which in English goes:

> Dance to your God
> Dance to your God
> Who else helps you
> when you languish in the bushes?

Eventually I was able to return to my home country and reunite with my parents, four brothers, and two sisters.

Though I was able to return to primary school at that time, I faced intense discrimination from my Hutu and Tutsi classmates, who believed I belonged in the forest as a sort of subhuman being, hunting and gathering as my people did for thousands of years. Most Batwa children couldn't bear the discrimination against them and dropped out; this continues today.

In sixth grade I found Christianity, and the poetry of the Bible has accompanied me ever since. Though most Burundian churches use the French Bible, I prefer the Kirundi, as its poetry resonates most resoundingly for me. I love the poetry of David, son of Jesse, especially his psalms of hope in the face of despair. I also am drawn to the Bible's poetry of despair over injustice, passages like Psalm 38, Lamentations 2–4, and the book of Jeremiah, which articulates the prophet's sadness because of the injustices of war that resulted in so many orphans.

Despite our communal despair, I still have faith in poetry, which I believe can make things happen, especially as an articulation of our deepest heartaches and longings, but also in a more direct way. Recently, a Burundian president instructed a provincial governor to give a Batwa community a parcel of their own land—the first step toward our alleviation of poverty. In a shrewd act the governor complied with the letter by allotting us a barren plot of land, useless for agricultural activity. As a form of protest, the Batwa community gathered at a large party with the president in attendance, singing:

Thank you, Mr. President
for giving us a plot
of dust and stones.

In response to the poetry of illiterates, our president addressed the situation and came to our aid, helping us acquire productive land.

Translated from the French and Kirundi by David Shook

Somehow we survive
and tenderness, frustrated, does not wither.
from "Somehow We Survive"

It was my turn. In memory of Damo and other victims of state violence, I read two poems by Langston Hughes and Ai, holding on to their words as to a raft in choppy waters.

Three kicks between the legs
That kill the kids
I'd make tomorrow.
from "Third Degree" by Langston Hughes

At some point, we will meet
at the tip of the bullet,
the blade, or the whip
as it draws blood,
but only one of us will change,
only one of us will slip
past the captain and crew of this ship
and the other submit to the chains
of a nation
that delivered rhetoric
in exchange for its promises.
from "Endangered Species" by Ai

As I read, I pictured Damo being tased (twice) by Chicago police and hitting his head so hard that he was brain-dead when he arrived at the hospital. Unable to adequately convey my horror, I borrowed the poet's tongue and took comfort in losing myself in another's words.

The gathering was titled "'No Knock,' an Artistic Speak-Out against 'the American Police State.'" The title was of course inspired by Gil Scott-Heron's poem "No Knock."

No knocked on my brother, Fred Hampton,
bullet holes all over the place!
No knocked on my brother, Michael Harris
and jammed a shotgun against his skull!

It is as it ever was. No knocked on Damo, who is now six feet underground.

Passersby stopped to listen as various people read poems about Guantanamo, police violence, prisons, surveillance, and more. Lorde is right: "Poetry is the way we help give name to the nameless so it can be thought. The farthest external horizons of our hopes and fears are cobbled by our poems, carved from the rock experiences of our daily lives."

There is magic in hearing voices speaking out for justice over the din of a bustling city. Gathering as a collective to recite poetry can't end state violence, but it can lift our spirits so that we might live another day to fight for more justice. Now more than ever we need words to help us think through that which cannot be thought. Poetry can help lift the ceiling from our brains so that we can imagine liberation.

ALEKSANDAR HEMON's most recent novel is *The Making of Zombie Wars*. He lives in Chicago.

SARAJEVO BLUES

I left Sarajevo in the winter of 1992, a couple of months before the siege began, and after some wandering I ended up in Chicago. When the war started, I watched the news and read the papers compulsively, for I needed every bit of information to understand what was going on in my hometown. But those stories were reductive and cold, aimed at the marginally interested American public, and not even the infrequent letters and phone calls from my friends and family could help me comprehend the situation. The letters were reluctant to complain, and the phone calls stuck to basic facts and gossip: who was killed, who was wounded, who went to the other side, only occasionally exposing me to the horror people lived in. I needed to know more—feeling intensely guilty for not being in Sarajevo, I needed to imagine fully what it was like to live and think and feel under the siege.

Then, sometime in 1995, toward the end of the war and siege, I received a small, thin chapbook with mimeographed pages, containing Semezdin Mehmedinović's *Sarajevo Blues*. Semezdin was a poet and a friend (and he still is both, I am happy to say), and I knew he had been writing and publishing intensely in the besieged city, as he was one of the many who believed that writing was an act of resistance in itself. But nothing prepared me for the fragment in *Sarajevo Blues* in which a mental patient, expelled from the institution by the besieging Serbs, accosts a passerby on the street, holding a dead sparrow by its claws, and says: "And you will be dead too, when my army arrives." Or a mother calling her child playing outside to come home, because "it is shelling outside," a call all the more poignant if you know that the mother was the poet's wife and the child his son.

Sarajevo Blues abounds in images and details that could only carelessly and callously be called surreal. What to those of us who lived (and still live) unbesieged might appear surreal was in fact hyperrealistic to the people in Sarajevo. Reality was under attack, its structure being altered. With a clear eye and an attentive ear, Semezdin parsed the new Sarajevo reality, patiently noting his discoveries in a combination of poems, prose fragments, and brief essays. The genre distinctions were collapsed because they couldn't really matter—everything was shattered into fragments, and those fragments had to be put together by any means necessary. At the epicenter of it all is a poet's consciousness, for only a poet—and a poet of Semezdin's caliber—could handle the fragmentary detail and the immensity of what was happening.

The precision of the detail, coupled with the awareness of what it all means, is everywhere in *Sarajevo Blues*. In "Animals," Semezdin writes: "I do not know how much longer I can bear a life like this. I get thrills every time, when at the thundering [of the artillery] outside, the cat snaps out of sleep and then, on my chest, I feel the slow unsheathing of her claws."

The sensory exactness of moments like this brought the siege home for me, quite literally, and made me comprehend what it was like to exist in Sarajevo. But *Sarajevo Blues* was not just bearing witness—although that would be admirably sufficient; it was also exposing the flimsy ways in which "our" reality ("we" being the unbesieged) is assembled to be comforting and bearable. For in the end, the central fact of every life is death, a fact that "we" choose to ignore for as long as possible. The purpose of "our" reality is to cover up the fact of death, and one of the things writers and poets can—and should—do is to unpack the lies of reality, beginning with the lie of life eternal in the present. What Semezdin did in *Sarajevo Blues*, with the heart and mind of a superb poet, was to recognize that the collapse of reality in Sarajevo was directly related to the ubiquity of death, which makes the city different from any other place on earth only in degree but not in kind. Nowhere is that more clear than in the poem called "Corpse":

> We slowed down at the bridge
> to watch dogs by the Miljacka

tearing apart a human corpse
then we went on

nothing in me has changed

I listened to the snow bursting under the tires
like teeth crunching an apple
and I felt a wild desire to laugh
at you
because you call this place hell
and you flee from here convinced
that death beyond Sarajevo does not exist

Reading *Sarajevo Blues*, I not only understood what it meant to live in Sarajevo under siege—I understood what it meant to live.

JEFFREY BROWN is senior correspondent for the PBS *NewsHour* and author of the poetry collection *The News*.

REPORTING POETRY

I am a correspondent for PBS *NewsHour*. That title conjures a certain style, tone, use of language, and subject matter. Every morning, we gather in a conference room and toss around events, names of people, places. The starting point: What happened? Then: What is most "important," most "compelling," most "interesting"? Finally: How to tell it?

I spend most days working with my colleagues to produce news stories—talking to experts and sources, reading clips and documents, looking at tapes, following the latest wires, writing questions and scripts. At the appointed hour I speak into a camera, read the copy, conduct the interviews. I tell it—what happened. Wars, natural disasters, elections, economic downturns, politicians, generals, CEOs—the news and the newsmakers you expect to see and hear.

But there is more to tell. January 2011: thirty men and women are crowded into a small, hot room in Carrefour, the sprawling poor "suburb" of Port-au-Prince, Haiti. Outside, an eerie landscape: enormous piles of rubble on every corner, gutted and wrecked houses (do people live in them?), pitted but now passable streets. It is a year since the earthquake that destroyed more than half the buildings in this area. Inside, a refuge, a celebration for lovers of words who have somehow made their way here from all over the area. They are poets, word struck and history stuck. ("In Haiti," the writer Evelyne Trouillot had told me, "people refer to history like it's yesterday.") Garnel Innocent, one of the poets, says: "We're just a bunch of crazy artists here. And we want to see what Haiti can become, then what Haiti will become."

This is the Bibliothèque Justin Lhérisson, not much of a "library" as we think of it, more a small community center where every Saturday for the past ten years or so, the "crazy artists" have come to meet one another, read their works, and hold classes in writing and painting. Occasionally one of the island's literary stars will come for a workshop. On this day there is much reciting, singing, shouting lines, sometimes back and forth, in Creole and French. I can make out references to the quake, cholera, hunger, death, but also to pleasure, fellowship, drinking, and love, love, love. A drummer joins in. The participants somehow know when to jump in, when to give way to the next one, and, finally, when to raise the volume as all recite at once, great piles of words and rhythm, louder and louder, faster and faster, and then done, as the poets of Justin Lhérisson dissolve into laughter, having performed their weekly homage to language, feeling, comradeship, no matter what has gone on outside. Coutechève Lavoie Aupont, one of the organizers of the gathering, tells me: "We're conscious of the image people say Haiti is projecting . . . It's only through culture and literature that we can question our problems as a nation and as human beings."

I was there as a reporter. What does it mean, to report? This is what we do every night on the news: give an account of the day. But it's a tricky thing to be *there* when you are not *of* there, to give a true account when the time and the understanding are so limited. So, yes, we accumulate facts and observations and then give *an* account.

What happened that day in Carrefour? In one tiny corner of Haiti, men and women gathered together to tell their histories, their lives, their hopes and joys, anger and sorrows. Poetry happened.

I report on poetry. In an age of chattering twenty-four-hour news of the latest celebrity this or that, it is barely conceivable. But it also makes a kind of sense. Literature has long provided me with a connection, a way in. I have seen the world, traveled the world through poetry and learned much from it of the power and process of giving an account.

Another day, many years earlier, in a classroom in California a professor greeted his new students, turned his back, and wrote a line on the blackboard. He wheeled around and asked: "Who can tell me what this says?" There was silence. He gave a sad smile: "How can you call yourself educated if you don't know ancient Greek?"

Almost laughably old school, yes, but effective on at least one very impressionable young fellow. The professor—it was Norman O. Brown—went on to spin a tale of gods and men, of Daphne fleeing Apollo, from myth into literature. I was enthralled. I went on to study that literature and language. Decades later, the latter is mostly gone. But so much—a connection between past and present through words and ideas—has remained. What happened that day in California? A world opened up. Poetry happened—to me.

Poetry, in fact, came first for me, a first accounting of what it means to be alive in this world. Journalism came later. Homer told of war, loss, and return in a tale that lasts and speaks to us because it is in some way true to our own experience, opens our imaginations to the lives of others, and is so thrillingly told.

> Now the earth
> grew stained with bright blood as men fell in death
> close to one another: Trojans, allies,
> and Danáäns, too, for they, too, bled,
> although far fewer died—each one remembering
> to shield his neighbor from the fatal stroke.
> So all fought on, a line of living flame.
>
> translated by Robert Fitzgerald

The Iliad is specific in detail (like the news) and yet somehow universal and timeless. It is not "reporting" as we think of it in our nightly broadcast. Describing the war in Syria, I will not look into a camera and tell of a "line of living flame." Yet ancient epic poetry still offers, perhaps, the most vivid account of war we have.

Walt Whitman—a journalist!—wrote the news of his day for the *Brooklyn Daily Eagle* and other publications and then wrote the news in verse of a place that had not previously existed—his America—for those who have wandered in it ever since. I was one of the wanderers (I like to think I still am), crisscrossing the continent, seeking, finding, losing, lost with Whitman: "But where is what I started for, so long ago? / And why is it yet unfound?"

Through the years, many other poets reached me with their accounts of external events and interior lives. And it continues to this day. Recently I read Alice Oswald's *Memorial*, a modern-day version of the *Iliad*, a "report" from the Trojan plain that is as fresh as my morning newspaper:

> The first to die was Protesilaus
> A focused man who hurried to darkness.

What journalist would not want to write a sentence as clean and clear as that? From early on, I have wanted that and more: to connect these often disconnected worlds of news and poetry, to make a place in the news for poetry.

To my continued amazement (and it must be said, with gratitude, in part through the support of the foundation that publishes this magazine) the search for this other "news," these other "newsmakers," has become part of my job description. My own private joke: I am the first and only "Senior Correspondent for Poetry" in nightly news.

At West Point I watched cadets soon to deploy to Iraq analyze lines of Tu Fu ("Snow scurries / In the coiling wind") and Wallace Stevens ("Nothing that is not there") and read poetry of war—Owen, Komunyakaa, and, yes, Homer. When I asked a question about the link between reading poetry and becoming a military officer, the debate that followed shook me with its rawness and clarity about what was to come for these young people. One cadet said, "Poetry is directly related to our function as a military officer because, at the bottom level, we're all here training to take lives. And that's a concept that you really can't approach without art, without some sort of deeper understanding of the human condition, which is exactly what poetry is."

A second responded, "That's a clumsy way to say that. We're not here to take lives and destroy things. Perhaps those are the tools of the army and the military, but really we're here to learn how to be leaders. And . . . poetry has a direct influence on how I think about leadership and how people view leadership."

Several years later, I wrote this:

> Those backpacks on the benches
> Caps on their hooks
>
> A stand to attention
> For the professor of poetry
>
> Who prepares today's lesson plan:
> Death and honor at Thermopylae
>
> Gettysburg and Hamburger Hill
> And the names we announce:

Baghdad, Fallujah, Najaf
Kabul, Khost, Korengal

Will reciting a sonnet
Make me a better lieutenant?

This is what they ask
With Shelley, with Owen

Measuring war by meter
Command by rhyme

Killing by form
Victory by the time

It takes to read one's way
From Troy to Kandahar

We're here, the cadet says
To learn to take lives

And art serves (we all serve)
An arc of humanity in death

The ancient brutality of battle
Muck and muse, books and blood

The most powerful tool
A soldier has, the general writes

Is not his weapon but his mind
And art—let us decide—

Can call forth what is best
Even as men do their worst

"West Point"

Discussions of the role of poetry in our society can feel irrelevant or abstract. Not in that West Point classroom. And not in a high-security Arizona prison where I watched the remarkable Richard Shelton lead a workshop for inmates. Most in the group—white, Latino, black, former gang members, skinheads—had never written before. One or two, including Andrew Jaicks, had years of writing under their belts and turned out accomplished work. (Jaicks jokingly put me in my place when I said, "It's nice to meet a prisoner who knows so much about poetry." He responded, "Well, it's nice to meet a *journalist* who knows something about poetry.") The critiques were gentle and respectful but direct. Another inmate, James Gastelum, told me: "This place isn't very conducive to truth, you know? . . . There's a lot of walls up. I know that Mr. Shelton, he'll tell you like it is."

Shelton himself later said to me that what the inmates get from poetry is an "attitude toward language, that if you can learn to use language honestly, then you can apply it to yourself honestly. And I think you can see yourself in a different light than you did before." It's an insight that has stayed with me. A lesson that applies whether one is in or out of prison.

There are many other stories and places. I recently witnessed children in a blighted Detroit neighborhood talk of W. S. Merwin's line on words hiding "inside this pencil" and then pick up their own pencils to write. Títos Patríkios, a Greek poet who lived through German occupation and then imprisonment and torture in the civil war that followed, spoke to me of the meaning of "austerity"—"an economic crisis always also creates other crises." Israeli and Palestinian poets told of the human costs of decades of violence and hatred. It was Taha Muhammad Ali, in his trinket shop in Nazareth, who said there are "two kinds of language, one for the news, for the politicians . . . and one for poetry . . . and they are different, very different languages."

He did his best, though, to reach people of all kinds. Another remarkable man.

Indeed, along the way, in this country and abroad, I met many of our finest, most insightful poets and writers. I asked questions about language, words, and lives that we all share. I learned over and over that the news comes from many directions, in many forms, that there are many ways—including a work of art, a piece of music, lines of poetry—to describe "what happened."

I confess I never liked Pound's famous statement that poetry is "news that stays news." Poetry is news, yes, sometimes the most profound news. But only some poetry—great poetry—will "stay news." Most won't. At the same time, some *news* will stay news. ("From Dallas, Texas, the flash, apparently official, President Kennedy died at 1:00 pm central standard time.") Most, indeed, should and will not.

The world in its dark grace.
I have tried to record it.
"A Short History of My Life," by Charles Wright

Each of us must come to terms with what he sees and what he will say. On that trip to Haiti in 2011, the nation's best-known poet, Frankétienne, surveying what he called a "dying country," told me, "Words cannot save the world." Look around you, see the destruction, the stupidity, the despair, and you have to believe he's right. And yet an account must be given: Frankétienne and the "crazy" poets of the Bibliothèque Justin Lhérisson continue to observe and write the news of the world. A journalist continues to report the news of the day.

RACHEL COHEN is author of *A Chance Meeting* and *Bernard Berenson: A Life in the Picture Trade*. Her essays have appeared in *Best American Essays* and the *Pushcart Prize Anthology*. She is a professor of practice in creative writing at the University of Chicago.

LIKE SOLDIERS MARCHING

My cousin Sophie, a cousin of my grandmother's, sometimes says to me that she wishes she knew someone who spoke Polish and who knew the poems she knows; she would just like to talk about poetry now and again. Once or twice she's told me of how her mother, gone these sixty years, used to read poetry aloud when Sophie was a girl. Sophie was quick with languages, has always been quick, first with Polish and then with the German of the camps, and after the war Swedish and English, then Hebrew in Israel, and English again in America. Polish, though, is the language of her family and childhood, and she was quickest with Polish. "I would read a poem once," she says, "and close my eyes and it would get organized in my head." There are a few pictures of her from that time, a girl with a kind of joyousness, her head up, alert, her angular arms flung out. She is still girlish and joyous and alert, though less angular in her age.

Sophie can still recite, in its entirety, a poem critical of the First World War by Bruno Jasienski written in an unusual pattern with just two syllables—"like soldiers marching," she says—on a line. She learned it one afternoon in the Warsaw ghetto. She was with her mother, and they were running from the Germans, who were blocking each street at both ends and then going through all the houses one by one. The two of them ran to the top floor of a building, where one of the apartments had a broken door. Sophie's mother thought the Germans might see the broken door and think the apartment had already been searched, so they went inside. The apartment still had its furniture. There was a book of poems open on the bed. "My mother thought I was crazy," Sophie said, "but I started reading. Never in my life have I wanted so much to just go into another country. I wanted to walk into that book. I memorized the poem.

The Germans were in the building—they threw a baby out a window, I saw a woman jump. I remember thinking 'A' is a shelter you can go into, 'M' is a bridge you can walk across."

The Warsaw ghetto was the last place she saw her parents and her younger brother, Stefan. From there, Sophie went into the camps, at fifteen, alone. She was in fourteen camps; she was in Majdanek and in Auschwitz and in Bergen-Belsen. At Bergen-Belsen they did no work, they were just kept—"they almost didn't feed us"—and lights-out was very early. "That was the time for poetry," Sophie says. In the evenings, lying on the boards they slept on all together, she recited poems, out loud, ones she remembered from school and from her mother. She has a high voice, unusually sweet, that has a little quaver in it. In English she always pronounces every letter in a word, which has the effect of seeming to recognize each word and to value it.

Once, some thirty years after the liberation of the camps, Sophie was working in the office of the United Nations Association in Washington, DC, where she was the executive director for many years, and a woman came by who had a Polish accent. They began to speak, and it transpired that they had both been in the camps, and in some of the same camps. "I thought so," said the woman, "you used to recite poetry at night, I recognized your voice."

"Poetry," Sophie says sometimes, "is how I kept my language. For years I had no one to speak Polish with, and I would sit and remember poems. The way I feel it is like pulling threads out of my mind, you pull a line and then you pull another line. That's how I still have my Polish. I was in touch with that lady for many years, but now I have no one who I can talk with about those poems of long ago."

PANKAJ MISHRA is an Indian novelist. He writes political essays for several publications, including the *New York Times*, the *New York Review of Books*, and *London Review of Books*.

RAMA STORES

In 1985, when I was sixteen years old, I left home to go to university in Allahabad, a provincial North Indian city. The university had been famous once, largely for providing a disproportionate share of elite civil servants to the Indian government. By the time I arrived there to do an undergraduate degree in commerce, students from the populous, poverty-stricken regions surrounding Allahabad had overwhelmed the university. It would be hard for most of these students to find even minor, ill-paid jobs, and many of them lingered around the university, sometimes for more than a decade, often drifting into criminality—contract murder, kidnapping, and extortion. North India's fractious caste politics alone seemed to offer some social mobility, and elections to the student union were bloody affairs, with regular shoot-outs between rival groups on and around the campus.

I kept my distance from this chaos. I knew I wanted to be a writer. The desire had developed early in my childhood. But, at sixteen, I still didn't know what I could write about. My small-town experience didn't seem worthy of extended literary treatment. I thought reading would stir up ideas; in Allahabad, sitting for hours in my small, darkened room, I devoured as many books as I could find or afford to buy at Wheelers, the only good bookshop in town, to which I cycled on most afternoons.

On the weekends I would take a train to the nearest British Council library. My roommate, who was preparing for the Civil Services examinations, loudly lamented my indifference to jobs and careers and predicted a penurious future for me. I had no trouble understanding the reasons for his mockery. I knew that reading books in English for the sake of reading was an absurd luxury in Allahabad. It was why I kept to myself my ambition of writing a novel in English, a language that no one around me spoke well, if at all.

In retrospect, the ambition may not seem presumptuous. By the mid-eighties, Indian novelists in English such as Salman Rushdie, Amitav Ghosh, and Vikram Seth had begun to publish. The success of *Midnight's Children* encouraged many aspiring writers in India. But the novel appeared difficult and largely alien to me, and I felt intimidated by its linguistic dazzle. The worlds Rushdie, Ghosh, and Seth described—Bombay, Egypt, California—were almost as remote as the worlds I encountered in the American or European novels that I was reading at the time. They could stoke my fantasies, but they offered no practical help to me in my own writing. In fact, their obvious glamour only heightened my anxiety that the world I lived in was not worth writing about.

Until they have been written about, things have no reality—or, at least, so it was for me in Allahabad. Only V. S. Naipaul, among writers in English, seemed to have seen the decaying, graffiti-ravaged buildings, the broken roads, the futile striving, and the blasted hopes around me. But I could not always enter his rage and anguish, which were those of the doubly displaced Indian. Kipling's Indian stories and R. K. Narayan's Malgudi fiction might have helped me, but I did not read them until much later. As it turned out, it was poetry that helped me find my material.

I read poetry for the same reason I read prose fiction: for a brief escape into a reality more comforting than the one I lived in. And I had read mostly European and American poets, untroubled by their alienness. The fact that I hadn't ever seen a daffodil made Wordsworth rather more attractive, and it is likely that if I had understood *The Waste Land* a bit more, I may have been puzzled by Eliot's aversion to the modern city—the place where I most wanted to be.

It was shocking and oddly exciting then to encounter a poem in English with the words "Rama Stores" in it. I used to pass this department store every time I cycled to Wheelers, and had thought nothing of it. To see the shop's name on a page suddenly made it appear interesting, even glamorous. I made a mental note of the poet's name: Arvind Krishna Mehrotra.

I learned that he lived in Allahabad. Not long afterward I began to notice him on the campus. With his long flowing white beard, he seemed to me a romantic figure, walking with a serene, casual air along the corridors of the English department, past the piles of broken furniture, to packed classrooms where, he would later tell me, students with no English would ask him to translate the Romantic poets into Hindi. I wondered then how he managed to transcend the severe discouragements that a writer or teacher of literature in Allahabad endured.

I would discover later that Mehrotra had, like me, spent much of his childhood in small towns, dreaming of writing. As a student in Bombay in the sixties, he had read and met other postcolonial Indian poets working in English: Nissim Ezekiel, Arun Kolatkar, Adil Jussawalla. As I discovered, these poets had not only infused ordinary, everyday life with poetic and philosophical meaning. They had also attempted themes—India's compromised modernity, existential alienation, urban poverty—and a range of tones and moods that are still rare in Indian prose writing in English. Living in Allahabad in the late sixties, Mehrotra tried to recreate some of Bombay's cosmopolitanism, and the irreverence of the American Beats he admired.

At Wheelers I found a collection of Mehrotra's poems, *Middle Earth*, and read it closely, always noticing with a frisson bits of my own reality in it. I read other Bombay poets. Encouraged by their example, I started work on my own novel. It was about a young man from the provinces who, lost and adrift in Bombay, uncovers the hypocrisy and shallowness of his rich relatives.

I sent a few initial pages along with a synopsis to Chatto & Windus, publishers in London. One day a reply came, expressing enthusiasm and wanting to see more. Over the following months I would open the envelope often, running my fingers over the embossed letterhead. I also mailed some pages to Mehrotra.

One afternoon my roommate appeared at the door and told me that a *dhadiwalla*, a man with a conspicuous beard, wanted to see me. Mehrotra was standing in the corridor, leaning against the balustrade, as I emerged from my room. I was overwhelmed, and could only nod when he suggested that we go to a nearby chai shack. There, after we had sat down and ordered tea, he started to talk, saying that he had liked what he read of my novel. We talked about other books, the kind I had been taking out from the British Council library, novels by Evelyn Waugh, Anthony Burgess, Graham Greene. He asked me if I wrote poems. (I didn't.) It was the first literary conversation I had ever had, much of it conducted, I recall, in English, a language I almost never spoke in Allahabad.

As we parted, Mehrotra invited me to his home. For weeks I thought of going. But shyness finally overcame me, and I would not visit his home until several years later. I also found myself unable to complete my novel. It is as though its sole purpose was to elicit encouragement, to tell me that it was worth continuing my quest to be a writer—the encouragement I first knew when I encountered the words "Rama Stores" in Mehrotra's poem and began to feel that I might have something to write about.

DR. OMAR KHOLEIF is the Manilow Senior Curator at the Museum of Contemporary Art Chicago and a visiting professor at the University of Chicago. He is the author or editor of over twenty books of narrative prose, art criticism, and fiction.

TO SPEAK WITH MANY TONGUES AT ONCE

I have always been an immigrant. I left Egypt, where I was born, at three months of age. I lived in the West as an Arab infant in exile. When I returned home as a teenager, I was a stranger to my own extended family who scoffed and giggled at my polyglot Arabic accent. Now that I am living in the United States again, I realize I have been code-switching my whole life: constantly attempting to assimilate, not only speaking but also writing in a foreign language, a tongue and vernacular not my own. I have watched the world devour the image of my people and their collective identities on many stages. I've been privy to everyone from presidents to schoolkids spewing bigoted rhetoric, seeing the Arabic-speaking world conflated with the violence of religious extremism, a condition created and spoon-fed to the public by political commentators who are perhaps oblivious to their own complicity in making history.

I've always longed to find a native polyglot like me, someone who could discuss the mutilation of the Arab image in the Western consciousness, with whom I could talk about Putin and Paris, Netanyahu and Nagasaki, Tehran and Tel Aviv. But increasingly, freedom of expression is stripped and buried in the Arab world—the young Egyptian author Ahmed Naji, for example, was recently sentenced to prison for writing novels that speak of sex and hashish. Egypt, the largest of Arab countries, is emulating the violently oppressive and homophobic Cuba that Reinaldo Arenas protested. With the November 2015 terrorist attacks in Paris, the image of the Muslim as well as the Arab became hollowed of any poetry.

There is one figure I keep returning to, one who eloquently captures the essence of this collective trauma, and that is the poet, essayist, and painter Etel Adnan. She was born in Beirut in 1925 to a Syrian father and a Greek mother from Smyrna. Adnan grew up in a household of multiple languages: Greek, Arabic, Turkish, and French, to name the ones that I am certain of. However, in her meditation on growing up, "To Write in a Foreign Language," Adnan explains how writing in English (as opposed to the many languages spoken in her familial home) became a form of resistance; she untangles the concept of home. Hers was a life lived in multiple self-imposed and forced exiles from the Arab world (specifically her native Beirut); she spent much of her life between Paris and the mountain ranges of Sausalito, California. In these places, Adnan worked in prose, poetry, and painting, merging these worlds into a tapestry of her imagination. Her works evoked a hybrid being—a creolized subject, persistently developing a sense of home in foreign lands.

In her collection *In the Heart of the Heart of Another Country*, Adnan negotiates memories of her native Lebanon. She begins:

> PLACE
> So I have sailed the seas and come . . .
> to B . . .
> a city by the sea, in Lebanon. It is seventeen years later. My absence has been an exile from an exile.

And she meditates:

> The most interesting things in Beirut are the absent ones. The absence of an opera house, of a football field, of a bridge, of a subway, and, I was going to say, of the people and the government. And, of course, the absence of absence of garbage.

Absence is a theme that recurs in *The Arab Apocalypse*, a book where hieroglyphic painted forms sit and breathe next to evocative passages of text. Here, Adnan reflects on the violently mediated and highly contested image of the Arab, who has become a loathed public enemy:

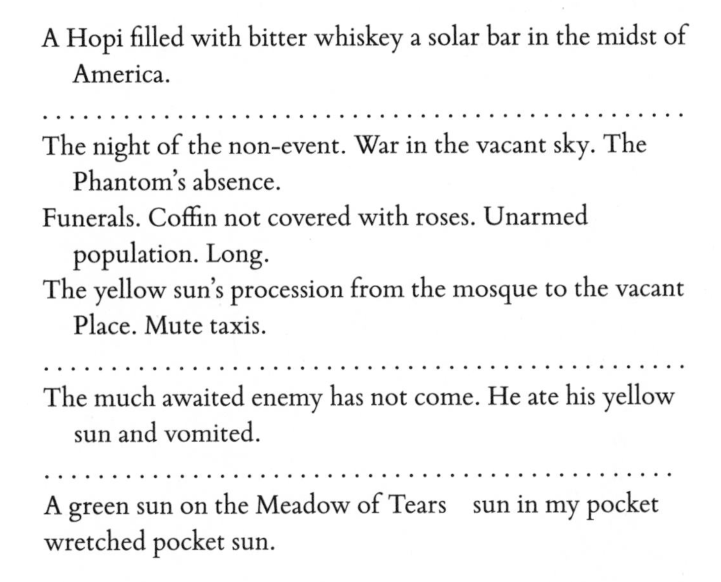

A Hopi filled with bitter whiskey a solar bar in the midst of
America.

. . . .

The night of the non-event. War in the vacant sky. The
Phantom's absence.
Funerals. Coffin not covered with roses. Unarmed
population. Long.
The yellow sun's procession from the mosque to the vacant
Place. Mute taxis.

. . . .

The much awaited enemy has not come. He ate his yellow
sun and vomited.

. . . .

A green sun on the Meadow of Tears   sun in my pocket
wretched pocket sun.

The sun is an embittered device that evokes, absorbs, and contains the trauma of Beirut after the Lebanese Civil War. The passage might be an allegory for the collective trauma ensnaring the nations of the Arab world since the collapse of the pan-Arab ideal in 1967. Yet Adnan's words are coping mechanisms, ways out of the alienation induced by diasporic Arab status. This is often most clearly evoked by her landscapes—written as poetry, and accompanied by her broad brushstroke paintings. In *Journey to Mount Tamalpais,* Adnan retreats from the burden of the past, seeking solace in the hills before her: "open wide the earth, shake trees from their roots." A kind of liberated renewal takes place: Adnan emancipates herself from the burden of being placeless (or indeed, of many nonplaces), claiming art as the site of her escape and shelter.

More recently she has conjured a new form of critical resolve in her treatise on love, which was first printed as a notebook for the art event Documenta 13, *The Cost for Love We Are Not Willing to Pay*.

> Love begins . . . becomes a desire to repeat the experience. It becomes an itinerary. A voyage. The imagination takes over that reality and starts building fantasies, dreams, projects . . . It creates its own necessity, and in some people encompasses the whole of life. . . .

How can one bear such an intensity? . . .

But what is love? And what are we giving up when we relinquish it?

Love is not to be described, it is to be lived. We may deny it, but we know it when it takes hold of us. When something in ourselves submits the self to itself.

Etel Adnan dances through language, speaking not only of many tongues but also of many places. Through her writing, the condition of exile becomes one of possible resistance.

CHRIS HEDGES was a war correspondent for nearly two decades. He is author of several books, including *War Is a Force That Gives Us Meaning*; *Days of Destruction, Days of Revolt* (with cartoonist Joe Sacco); and *Wages of Rebellion: The Moral Imperative of Revolt*.

HOW WITH THIS RAGE

I have spent most of my adult life in war. I began in Central America during the civil wars in El Salvador and Nicaragua, where I spent five years; on to the Middle East, where I spent seven; and ended my career in the besieged city of Sarajevo and finally Kosovo. My life has been marred, let me say deformed, by the organized industrial violence that year after year was an intimate part of my existence. I have looked into the eyes of mothers keening over the mutilated and lifeless bodies of their children on dusty roads in Central America and cobblestone squares in Sarajevo. I have stood in warehouses with rows of corpses, including children, and breathed death into my lungs. I carry within me the ghosts of my comrades now gone.

Where do you turn in the midst of a world bent on self-annihilation, a world where lives are snuffed out at random? Whom do you reach for to keep from disintegrating under the pressure, the carnage, and the loneliness? Who speaks to you in such trance-like misery?

To a certain extent, no one. All of us who have been in war bear with us memories we would prefer to bury or forget. War has an otherworldliness, a strangeness unlike most other experiences. It is its own culture. It infects everything around it, even humor, which is preoccupied with the grim perversities of smut and death. Such tragedy, such inexplicable cruelty, banishes all vague generalizations about existence and obliterates ideological constructs. The fundamental questions about the meaning, or meaninglessness, of our existence are laid bare when we sink to the lowest depths.

But war is fundamental to the human condition. Will Durant calculated that there have been only twenty-nine years in all of human history during which a war was not underway somewhere. Rather than an aberration, war exposes a side of human nature that is masked by the often unacknowledged coercion and constraints that glue us together. Our cultivated conventions and little lies of civility lull us into a refined and idealistic view of ourselves. "The gallows," the gravediggers in *Hamlet* aptly remind us, "is built stronger than the church."

From the time I began covering war I have carried with me books that are my refuge. Some of the writers include the obvious: Homer, William Shakespeare, Wilfred Owen, W. H. Auden, T. S. Eliot, George Orwell, Joseph Conrad. Also Marcel Proust, whose *In Search of Lost Time* carried me for many weeks through the war in Bosnia. All these poets and writers understood the monstrous indifference of nature. They understood the dark forces within us, the Hobbesian universe born out of violence and chaos. Great writing serves as a steady reminder that, among mutable and inconstant human beings, there remain glimpses of redemption, understanding, and compassion—even if these virtues rarely triumph.

Reading great poems, novels, and essays helps us to cope with our own insecurities and uncertainty, allowing us to plunge to the very depths of our inner being, depths that often lie beyond articulation. These writers help us to define ourselves and give words to grief and pain and joy that would otherwise lie beyond our reach. And reading like this saves us from the deadening textual criticism and academic snobbery that overpowers and destroys the heart and soul of great art.

"As long as reading is for us the instigator whose magic keys have opened the door to those dwelling-places deep within us that we would not have known how to enter, its role in our lives is salutary," Proust wrote. "It becomes dangerous, on the other hand, when, instead of awakening us to the personal life of the mind, reading tends to take its place."

Late one night, unable to sleep during the war in El Salvador, I picked up *Macbeth*. It was not a calculated decision. I had come that day from a village where about a dozen people had been murdered by the death squads, their thumbs tied behind their backs with wire and their throats slit.

The play, read in this light, took on a new power. The thirst for power at the cost of human life was no longer an abstraction. I came upon Macduff's wife's speech, made when the murderers, sent by

Macbeth, arrive to kill her and her small children. "Whither should I fly?" she asks.

> I have done no harm. But I remember now
> I am in this earthly world, where to do harm
> Is often laudable, to do good sometime
> Accounted dangerous folly.

These words seized me like Furies. They cried out for the dead I had seen lined up that day in a dusty market square, the dead I have seen since: the three thousand children who were killed in Sarajevo, the dead who lie in unmarked mass graves in Bosnia, Kosovo, Iraq, the Sudan, and Algeria, the dead who are my own, who carried notebooks, cameras, and a vanquished idealism into war and never returned. Of course resistance is usually folly, of course power exercised with ruthlessness will win, of course force easily crushes gentleness, compassion, and decency.

But these words give me a balm to my grief, a momentary solace, a little understanding, as I stumble forward into the void.

ACKNOWLEDGMENTS

The editors acknowledge and thank our authors, their representatives, and the *Poetry* magazine, Poetry Foundation, and University of Chicago Press staff for their role in creating this anthology, especially

Carrie Olivia Adams
Holly Amos
Danielle Chapman
Sarah Dodson
Lindsay Garbutt
Ruth Goring
Margaret Hivnor
Nathan Hoks
Valerie Jean Johnson
Helen Lothrop Klaviter
Christina Pugh
Gina Rosemellia
Scott Stealey
Elizabeth Stigler
Adam Travis
Alan G. Thomas
Christian Wiman
Serene Yang

CONTRIBUTORS

LYNDA BARRY is a cartoonist and writer. She has authored twenty-one books and received numerous awards and honors. Her book *One! Hundred! Demons!* was required reading for all incoming freshmen at Stanford University in 2008. She is an associate professor of interdisciplinary creativity and director of the Image Lab at the University of Wisconsin–Madison.

NAOMI BECKWITH holds degrees from Northwestern University and the Courtauld Institute of Art in London. She is the Marilyn and Larry Fields Curator at the Museum of Contemporary Art in Chicago and focuses on conceptual practices in contemporary art, especially work that engages discourses of blackness. She has curated several exhibitions in the United States and internationally. In 2015 she cocurated, with Dieter Roelstraete, *The Freedom Principle*, an exhibit that explored art and music from Chicago's South Side from the midsixties to the present.

JERRY BOYLE is a civil litigation attorney who works for Alvin W. Block & Associates in Chicago. He works pro bono on cases involving activism, free speech, and public demonstrations. Hailing from a large family of Irish lawyers, Boyle is a member of the National Lawyers Guild. Along with other members of the Guild, he was on hand to work as a legal observer during the demonstrations and police activity at the 2016 Republican National Convention in Cleveland, Ohio.

JEFFREY BROWN grew up in Belmont, Massachusetts. Currently a senior correspondent for the *PBS NewsHour*, Brown worked early in his career for the Columbia University Seminars on Media and Society, producing public television programs on political topics. In 1988 he began working as an economics reporter for *The MacNeil/Lehrer NewsHour*. His poetry collection *The News* was published in 2015.

NEKO CASE began her career as a singer and songwriter in the Pacific Northwest, playing drums for various punk bands in the early nineties. Case recently released an eight-album vinyl box set of her complete solo discography titled *Truckdriver, Gladiator, Mule*. She also performs with Canadian-bred rock band The New Pornographers.

RACHEL COHEN is a nonfiction writer and professor at the University of Chicago. She is the author of *A Chance Meeting* and *Bernard Berenson: A Life in the Picture Trade*. She has written for publications such as the *New Yorker*, the *Believer*, the *Threepenny Review*, and the *London Review of Books*, and is the recipient of a Guggenheim Fellowship for her writing about art. Sophie Degan is, at ninety, still reading and translating poetry.

ROGER EBERT (1942–2013) was an acclaimed journalist and film critic for the *Chicago Sun-Times*. He covered sports for the *Daily Illini* as a student at the University of Illinois in the early sixties and began his career as a film critic while a PhD student at the University of Chicago in 1967. He gave up his graduate work and went on to become the first film critic to win the Pulitzer Prize for Criticism in 1975.

HELEN FISHER is a biological anthropologist, a Senior Research Fellow at the Kinsey Institute, a member of the Center for Human Evolutionary Studies in the Department of Anthropology at Rutgers University, and chief scientific advisor to Match.com. Fisher uses fMRI brain scanning, as well as evolutionary and cross-cultural data, to understand human romantic love and attachment and current trends in human family life. Her six books include *Anatomy of Love*, *Why We Love*, and *Why Him? Why Her?*

MATT FITZGERALD is the senior pastor of Saint Pauls United Church of Christ in Chicago, one of the oldest churches in the city and one of the first congregations in the United States to affirm, welcome, and marry LGBTQ Christians. He hosts *Christian Century* magazine's award-winning *Preachers on Preaching* podcast and is a regular contributor to the *Stillspeaking Daily Devotional*. He lives in Chicago with his family.

LEOPOLD FROEHLICH worked for *Forbes* early in his journalism career. In 1991 he joined *Playboy* as copy chief and eventually became managing editor, leaving the magazine in 2013. He is currently senior editor at *Lapham's Quarterly* in New York City.

AMY FRYKHOLM is a Colorado-based writer and editor of the media column at the *Christian Century*. She holds a PhD in literature from Duke University and is currently at work on a book about the seventh-century desert saint Mary of Egypt. Frykholm has described her writing as dialogic, involving dialogue with her subjects so that other voices speak through her writing. She is the author of four books of nonfiction, including *Rapture Culture: Left Behind in Evangelical America*, *Julian of Norwich: A Contemplative Biography*, and *See Me Naked: Stories of Sexual Exile in American Christianity*.

ROXANE GAY is author of *Ayiti*, *An Untamed State*, and the best-selling *Bad Feminist*. A founding editor of the literary journal *Pank* and of Tiny Hardcore Books, a small press dedicated to publishing small-format books, Gay is a professor of English at Purdue University and an opinion writer for the *New York Times*.

DANIEL HANDLER is the author of six novels, including *Why We Broke Up,* which won a Michael L. Printz Honor, the national best seller *We Are Pirates*, and the forthcoming *All the Dirty Parts*. As Lemony Snicket, he is responsible for numerous books for children, including the thirteen-volume *A Series of Unfortunate Events,* the four-volume *All the Wrong Questions,* and *The Dark,* which won the Charlotte Zolotow Award. Handler continues to serve as the adjunct accordionist for the Magnetic Fields, among other musical projects, and he serves as executive producer and writer for the Netflix production of *A Series of Unfortunate Events*. He lives in San Francisco with the illustrator Lisa Brown, to whom he is married and with whom he has collaborated on several books and one son.

CHRIS HEDGES is a journalist, activist, and ordained Presbyterian minister who is currently a columnist for *Truthdig*, a progressive journal of news and opinion. He began his career as a war correspondent, reporting on the Falklands War from Argentina for National Public Radio. He has published several books, including *Death of the Liberal Class*, *Empire of Illusion: The End of Literacy and the Triumph of Spectacle*, and the best-selling *American Fascists: The Christian Right and the War on America*. His book *War Is a Force That Gives Us Meaning* was a finalist for the National Book Critics Circle Award for Nonfiction. He was part of a team of *New York Times* reporters who were awarded a Pulitzer Prize in 2002 for their coverage of global terrorism.

ALEKSANDAR HEMON was born in Sarajevo but has lived in the United States since the outbreak of the Bosnian War in 1992. He learned English as an adult and published his first short story in English in 1995. Hemon's acclaimed works of fiction include *The Question of Bruno*, *Nowhere Man*, *The Lazarus Project*, and *The Making of Zombie Wars*. Hemon has been awarded a Guggenheim and a MacArthur Fellowship. He lives in Chicago.

CHRISTOPHER HITCHENS (1949–2011) was a journalist and columnist who wrote for magazines such as *New Statesman*, the *Nation*, *Slate*, and *Vanity Fair*, covering topics both global and domestic. He advocated ardently for his notion of antitheism, which in his terms emphasized relief "that there is no evidence" for the existence of gods. He often sparked controversy over his public positions, such as his criticism of Mother Teresa's expansion of Catholic fundamentalism and his support for the Iraq War. Hitchens published several books, including *Cyprus*, *The Missionary Position: Mother Teresa in Theory and Practice*, *God Is Not Great: How Religion Poisons Everything*, and *Arguably: Essays*, winner of the 2012 PEN/Diamonstein-Spielvogel Award for the Art of the Essay.

JOLIE HOLLAND is an American songwriter, bandleader, multi-instrumentalist, singer, performer, and author. Her albums include *The Living and the Dead*, *Pint of Blood*, and *Wine Dark Sea*. In a review on National Public Radio, critic Stephen Thompson lauded her music for combining blues, rock, jazz, and soul into "a sound that lands halfway between dusty rural Americana and grimy New York art-rock." Holland writes an advice column on her website.

KAY REDFIELD JAMISON is a clinical psychologist who specializes in mood disorders, especially bipolar illness. Her writing has been widely influential in both academic and public settings, raising awareness of mental illnesses that often go untreated. Her books include *Nothing Was the Same: A Memoir*, *Exuberance: The Passion for Life*, and *Night Falls Fast: Understanding Suicide*. A 2001 MacArthur Fellow, Jamison is a professor of psychiatry at the Johns Hopkins School of Medicine. Her most recent book is *Robert Lowell, Setting the River on Fire: A Study of Genius, Mania, and Character*.

XENI JARDIN worked as a web developer before starting a career in journalism in 1999. She is a journalist and commentator on digital media, appearing on popular TV news stations such as CNN, MSNBC, and Fox News. She is a founding partner and coeditor of the blog *Boing Boing* and is executive producer and host of the Webby-honored *Boing Boing Video*.

TRACEY JOHNSTONE is a midwife, poet, human-rights activist, and author of legislation for the regulation of midwifery.

MARIAME KABA is an organizer, educator, and curator whose work focuses on ending violence, dismantling the prison industrial complex, and supporting youth leadership development. She is the founder and director of Project NIA, a grassroots organization with the long-term goal of ending youth incarceration. After spending twenty years based in Chicago, Kaba has returned to New York City, her hometown.

ROB KENNER is a music journalist who lives in New York City. His reviews and articles appear in the *New York Times*, National Public

Radio, *Complex*, *Mass Appeal*, and *Billboard*. He is the founder and publisher of *Boomshots*, an online mixed-media platform that publishes news, commentary, and interviews on reggae, dancehall, rap, and related musical genres. Kenner is also the author of a forthcoming history of reggae's worldwide impact.

OMAR KHOLEIF is a writer and the Manilow Senior Curator at the Museum of Contemporary Art Chicago. He is the author or editor of over twenty books of narrative prose, art criticism, and fiction, including *You Are Here: Art After the Internet*, *Moving Image*, *Fear Eats the Soul*, *How to Be Brown in America*, and *Goodbye World!* A specialist in modern and contemporary art, Kholeif is also a scholar of contemporary artist film, video, and emerging technology, with a particular focus on politics, narrative, and geography in a global context. Kholeif was born in Egypt and spent a large portion of his career in England, where he was a curator at the Whitechapel Gallery.

WILLIAM JAMES LENNOX JR. is a retired US Army three-star lieutenant general. After graduating from West Point, he served various assignments in the field artillery and held a number of staff positions, including a White House Fellowship as special assistant to the secretary of education. Lennox became the fifty-sixth superintendent of the United States Military Academy at West Point in 2001. He holds a PhD in literature from Princeton University and is currently the president of Saint Leo University.

IAIN MCGILCHRIST is a psychiatrist and philosopher who lives off the coast of northwest Scotland on the Isle of Skye. His work argues that the mind and brain can be understood only within the broad contexts of our physical and spiritual existence and of the wider human culture in which they arise. McGilchrist studied English at Oxford, but a lifelong interest in philosophy led him to train in medicine, later conducting research in neuroimaging at John Hopkins. He is a Quondam Fellow of All Souls College, Oxford; a Fellow of the Royal College of Psychiatrists; a Fellow of the Royal Society of Arts; and a former consultant psychiatrist and clinical director at the Bethlem Royal and Maudsley Hospital, London. His most recent publication is *The Master and His Emissary: The Divided*

Brain and the Making of the Western World. A feature film on his work is due for release in 2017.

PANKAJ MISHRA is a writer who was born in North India. After moving to Mashobra, a Himalayan village, in 1992, Mishra began writing reviews and essays for various Indian publications. His first book, *Butter Chicken in Ludhiana: Travels in Small Town India*, described the cultural effects of globalization in India. He has published eight books, most recently *Age of Anger: A History of the Present*. A recipient of the 2014 Windham-Campbell Prize for nonfiction, Mishra also writes political essays for the *New York Times*, the *New York Review of Books*, the *Guardian*, the *New Yorker*, and the *London Review of Books*.

ALFRED MOLINA is an English actor who was born in London to an Italian mother and a Spanish father. Molina made his film debut as Indiana Jones's guide in *Raiders of the Lost Ark*. He has appeared in many British and American television programs and stage productions. He is best known for his roles in films such as *Maverick*, *Spider-Man 2*, *Chocolat*, *The Da Vinci Code*, *An Education*, *Rango*, and *Prince of Persia: The Sands of Time*.

MOMUS is the artist name of the Scottish musician Nick Currie. Since the early eighties Momus has been releasing singer-songwriter albums on independent labels. The *Guardian* called him "the David Bowie of the art-pop underground." In the nineties he started blogging in various forms, and he has written journalism about technology, art, and design. He has published books of speculative fiction and appeared as a performance artist offering "unreliable tours" and "emotional lectures." He lives in Osaka, Japan.

NATALIE Y. MOORE is a reporter for WBEZ, Chicago's National Public Media station. She joined the station in 2007 after working as a reporter for the *Detroit News*, the *St. Paul Pioneer Press*, and the Associated Press in Jerusalem. Moore is coauthor of the books *Deconstructing Tyrone: A New Look at Black Masculinity in the Hip-Hop Generation* and *The Almighty Black P Stone Nation: The Rise, Fall, and Resurgence of an American Gang*. Her latest book is *The South Side: A Portrait of Chicago and American Segregation*.

NALINI NADKARNI is an ecologist who conducted groundbreaking research on Costa Rican rain forest canopies in the eighties. She continues to study the effects of forest fragmentation on biodiversity and community function, especially in her field sites in Costa Rica and Washington State. Nadkarni also participates in several outreach efforts to present research results to nonscientific audiences, including artists, faith-based groups, urban youth, and incarcerated men and women. She is a professor of biology at the University of Utah, the author of *Between Earth and Sky: Our Intimate Connections to Trees*, and coeditor of *Forest Canopies* and *Monteverde: Ecology and Conservation of a Tropical Cloud Forest*.

ETIENNE NDAYISHIMIYE is a former Batwa parliamentarian in the East Central African nation of Burundi. As a child he was forced to flee Burundi due to its civil war, living as a refugee for three years in the Democratic Republic of the Congo. Founder of UNIPROBA, a human rights nonprofit advocating for Batwa equality, he also mentors many young Batwa leaders.

ANDERS NILSEN has published eight books of comics and graphic narrative, including *Big Questions*, *The End*, and *Poetry is Useless*, as well as the coloring book *A Walk in Eden*. He has received three Ignatz Awards, a small-press comics prize, and the Lynd Ward Graphic Novel Prize. Nilsen currently resides in Portland, Oregon.

WILL OLDHAM writes and records songs under the stage name Bonnie "Prince" Billy and has been widely admired for his music's unique combination of Carnatic, country, and punk. Oldham had originally pursued an acting career, moving to Los Angeles in the late eighties and performing the role of Miles in *Thousand Pieces of Gold*. He has released over fifteen albums, most recently *Best Troubadour*. He has also collaborated with many artists, including The Cairo Gang, Dawn McCarthy, Mike Aho, Zach Galifianakis, and Kanye West.

FERNANDO PEREZ is a retired professional baseball player. He was an outfielder for the Tampa Bay Rays, appearing in the 2008 World Series. Perez now works as an instructor at the School of the New York Times and as a correspondent for *VICE*.

MICHAELANNE PETRELLA is coauthor of the children's book *Recipe*, which she wrote with her sister Angela Petrella. She lives in the San Francisco Bay Area and writes for *McSweeney's*.

NICHOLAS PHOTINOS is the founding cellist of the four-time Grammy Award–winning new music ensemble Eighth Blackbird. Formed in 1996, the ensemble tours throughout the world and has been featured at the 2013 Grammy Awards, on CBS's *Sunday Morning* and *Bloomberg TV*, and in the *New York Times*. The ensemble holds an ongoing ensemble-in-residence position at the University of Richmond. Eighth Blackbird began their own annual summer festival, the Blackbird Creative Lab, in Ojai, California, in 2017, the same year they won Chamber Music America's inaugural Visionary Award and were named Musical America's Ensemble of the Year. On his own, Photinos has performed and recorded with artists such as Björk, Wilco, and The Autumn Defense, and jazz artists such as violinist Zach Brock, bassist Matt Ulery, and singer Grazyna Auguscik. He has recorded for numerous labels, including Cedille, Nonesuch, and Naxos. His first solo album, *Petits Artéfacts*, is on the New Amsterdam label. He also teaches each summer at the Bang on a Can Summer Festival in North Adams, Massachusetts.

ARCHIE RAND is a Brooklyn-based artist whose work is displayed around the world. His murals have been commissioned by several synagogues, including the B'nai Yosef Synagogue in Brooklyn and Anshe Emet Synagogue in Chicago. Rand has also produced collaborative work with poets, including John Ashbery, Bill Berkson, Clark Coolidge, Robert Creeley, Bob Holman, David Lehman, Lewis Warsh, and John Yau. Rand's works are included in the collections of the Metropolitan Museum of Art, the Museum of Modern Art (MoMA), the Whitney Museum, the San Francisco Museum of Modern Art, the Art Institute of Chicago, the Victoria and Albert Museum, the Bibliothèque nationale de France, and the Tel Aviv Museum of Art. He is currently Presidential Professor of Art at Brooklyn College.

RICHARD RAPPORT is a clinical professor of neurosurgery at the University of Washington's School of Medicine and is an attending physician at Harborview Medical Center in Seattle. His research primarily focuses on the surgical management of epilepsy, anticonvulsant drugs, and the localization of speech and language. Rapport has been involved in issues of social justice, and his literary essays are seen widely in various forms. Several of his nearly forty published essays have been nominated for the Pushcart Prize, and one was noted in *Best American Essays*. He is the author of *Nerve Endings: The Discovery of the Synapse* and *Physician: The Life of Paul Beeson*. He lives in Seattle with his wife, the writer Valerie Trueblood.

CHE "RHYMEFEST" SMITH is a writer, activist, teacher, and hip-hop artist from Chicago's South Side. He has released three solo albums and shared cowriting credits on several songs, including Kanye West's "Jesus Walks," which won a Grammy in 2005. Smith took a break from music in order to become more politically active in Chicago. He ran for the Chicago City Council in 2011, narrowly losing in a runoff to the incumbent alderman. Along with Kanye West and Donnie Smith, he cofounded Donda's House in 2013. The nonprofit arts program provides art instruction to youth in at-risk communities.

RICHARD RORTY (1931–2007) was an important American philosopher best known for revitalizing the school of American pragmatism. Rorty was born in New York City to a politically active family and educated at the University of Chicago and Yale University. He served as a professor emeritus of comparative literature at Stanford and was the author of several books, including *Philosophy and the Mirror of Nature*, in which he articulated one of his core positions, a critique of the long-held assumption that knowledge "mirrors" the natural world.

ALEX ROSS has been the music critic of the *New Yorker* since 1996. His first book, *The Rest Is Noise: Listening to the Twentieth Century*, won a National Book Critics Circle Award and the Guardian First Book Award and was a finalist for the Pulitzer Prize. His second book is the essay collection *Listen to This*. He is now at work on *Wagnerism: Art in the Shadow of Music*. Ross has received an Arts and Letters Award from the American Academy of Arts and Letters, the Belmont Prize in Germany, a Guggenheim Fellowship, and a MacArthur Fellowship.

FRED SASAKI edits *Poetry* magazine's prose feature The View from Here, from which the essays in this book are gathered. He is the art director of *Poetry* magazine and a gallery curator at the Poetry Foundation. He authored *Real Life Emails*, a book of deluded emails, and the zine series *FRED SASAKI'S AND FRED SASAKI'S FOUR-PAGER GUIDE TO: HOW TO FIX YOU.* In 2004 he founded the Chicago Printers Ball, an annual celebration of poetry and printmaking. He is also cofounder of the Homeroom 101 pop and subculture show.

MARY SCHMICH is a Pulitzer Prize–winning columnist for the *Chicago Tribune* and wrote the *Brenda Starr* comic strip from 1985 to 2011. She also teaches yoga, plays mandolin and piano, and, with fellow columnist Eric Zorn, hosts an annual holiday musical event in Chicago to raise money for the Chicago Tribune Holiday Giving charity fund.

DON SHARE is the editor of *Poetry* magazine. Among his twelve books are *Wishbone*, *Union*, and *Bunting's Persia*; he also edited a critical edition of Basil Bunting's poems, named a Book of the Year by the *Times of London* and the *New Statesman*. *Miguel Hernández*, his book of translations, was awarded the Times Literary Supplement Translation Prize and Premio Valle Inclán. Other books of his include *Seneca in English*, *Squandermania*, and *The Open Door: 100 Poems, 100 Years of "Poetry" Magazine*. He received a VIDA "VIDO" Award for his contributions to American literature and literary community.

LILI TAYLOR is a stage and screen actress who starred in the indie classic *Mystic Pizza*. She has had roles in many films, including *Dogfight*, *Short Cuts*, and *I Shot Andy Warhol*. Taylor has also appeared in a number of Broadway plays, including *The Three Sisters*.

HANK WILLIS THOMAS is a photo conceptual artist working primarily with themes related to identity, history, and popular culture. Thomas's monograph *Pitch Blackness* was published by Aperture. He has exhibited throughout the United States and abroad and is in numerous public collections, including the Museum of Modern Art (MoMA), the Solomon R. Guggenheim Museum, and the National

Gallery of Art in Washington, DC. Collaborative projects include *Question Bridge: Black Males* and *In Search of the Truth* with Cause Collective. In 2015 Thomas cofounded For Freedoms, the first artist-run super Pac. Thomas is a member of the Public Design Commission for the city of New York. He received a BFA in Photography and Africana studies from New York University and his MFA/MA in Photography and Visual Criticism from the California College of Arts. Thomas is represented by Jack Shainman Gallery in New York City and Goodman Gallery in South Africa.

SALLY TIMMS is a singer-songwriter who has been a member of the Mekons since 1985. She grew up in the Yorkshire Dales, singing in her church choir and performing at competitive poetry recitals as a child. Timms recorded her first solo album, *Hangahar* (an experimental, improvised film score), at the age of nineteen with Pete Shelley of the Buzzcocks. Along with her work with the Mekons, she has released several solo albums, including *Cowboy Sally's Twilight Laments for Lost Buckaroos* on the alternative-country label Bloodshot Records. She lives in Chicago.

JIA TOLENTINO is a staff writer for the *New Yorker* website and formerly was the deputy editor of *Jezebel* and a contributing editor at the *Hairpin*. She writes on a range of subjects, from music reviews to gender and identity politics. Her essays and criticism have appeared in the *New York Times Magazine*, *Pitchfork*, and many other places.

JOSH WARN is a retired member of Ironworkers Local Union 25, Detroit, who still occasionally works in the steel industry, and in public schools as a substitute teacher. In addition to memorizing poetry, he loves canoeing Michigan rivers and lakes. He volunteers in religious and social justice organizations. Curiosity has led him to research and publish articles about topics in Michigan history and the fascinating year 1919. Late in life he discovered the joy and satisfaction of singing in a choir, where the choir members tolerate him.

AI WEIWEI is an artist who resides and works in both Berlin and Beijing. His father, the poet Ai Qing, was denounced by China's Communist Party in 1958, and his family was sent to labor camps, first near the North Korean border and then eventually in Xinjiang province. They returned to Beijing in 1976 after the end of the Cultural Revolution. Ai studied animation at the Beijing Film Academy, then studied art in New York in the early eighties. Upon returning to China a decade later, Ai advocated for experimental artists by publishing underground books and curating avant-garde exhibitions. He has worked in many media, including sculpture, installation, photography, architecture, and film. Ai is an outspoken advocate of human rights and freedom of speech. He received the Václav Havel Prize for Creative Dissent in 2012 and the Amnesty International Ambassador of Conscience Award in 2015.

STEPHEN T. ZILIAK is an economist who pioneered "haiku economics." He is known for his work on statistics, including the critically acclaimed book *The Cult of Statistical Significance* and numerous essays on Guinnessometrics, the scientific and statistical legacy of William S. Gosset, Guinness's Oxford-educated brewmaster. Ziliak is professor of economics and faculty member of the Social Justice Studies Program at Roosevelt University, professor of business and law at the University of Newcastle, faculty affiliate in the Graduate Program of Economics at Colorado State University, and faculty member of the Angiogenesis Foundation.